The
Most Common Mistakes
in
English Usage

The Most Common Mistakes *in* English Usage

THOMAS ELLIOTT BERRY

Professor of English
West Chester State College
West Chester, Pennsylvania

Boston, Massachusetts   Burr Ridge, Illinois
Dubuque, Iowa   Madison, Wisconsin   New York, New York
San Francisco, California   St. Louis, Missouri

McGraw-Hill

A Division of The McGraw·Hill Companies

The Most Common Mistakes in English Usage

First McGraw-Hill Paperback Edition, 1971
Originally published by Chilton Book Company, 1961

Copyright © 1961 by Thomas Elliott Berry

Library of Congress Catalog Card Number: 61-15418

07-005053-8

32 33 34 35 36 37 38 39 BKM BKM 0 9 8 7 6 5 4 3 2 1

Preface

This book has been written (1) to serve as an analysis of the errors most commonly made in spoken and written English and (2) to present clear explanations of how to correct these errors. It has also been prepared as a reference work for the general reader who may want to check questions of usage. Therefore, the book can be used either as a text or a handbook — as individual circumstances may decree.

As one peruses this book, he may well ask, "By what right does an author of a book on usage tell me how to speak and write?" The answer is that most authors in the field of usage do not dictate to their readers. Rather, they present, as this author has done, the guidelines for usage which are currently being observed by the most competent and careful speakers and writers. Thus the authors say to their readers, "Here are the principles of usage which are necessary for acceptable expression in educated society."

From the above discussion, one can see that the term "correct usage" — as used in this and similar books — must be equated with "usage of the linguistically competent"; that is, the term "correct" must be construed to mean the "language practices of those persons whose usage, in the opinion of language specialists, merits respect."

After reflecting upon this explanation of "correct" usage, one must recognize another fundamental fact: some questions of usage cannot be settled unequivocally in terms of "right" or "wrong." The reasons are quite clear. In some instances, specialists find that competent users of English differ in their observance of a given practice—e.g., the splitting of the infinitive. In other instances, specialists find that a practice widely endorsed in recent years is now disappearing—e.g., the fine distinctions between the use of "shall" and "will." In still other instances, they find situations that lie beyond any detailed analysis—e.g., the line between slang (which is a term, incidentally, that defies precise definition) and "acceptable" usage. As a result, no reputable specialist dare proclaim final rulings on many practices.

However, despite the fact that correct usage is, in a sense, an arbitrary and sometimes an unsettled matter, certain standards do exist; and the careful user of English must abide by them. These are the standards upon which this author bases his compilation of the "most common mistakes in English usage."

In attempting to master standards of usage, one should begin with the realization that he is engaging in a fascinating study. From the first lessons, one can find in learning principles of usage an exciting challenge —a challenge that actually makes pleasant the pursuit of the frequently disparaged "rules of grammar." One can derive herein the same fascination he encounters in examining the meaning and the application of federal, state, and local laws; and he can experience the same thrill he feels in learning the basic principles of chemistry, physics, and other disciplines.

In studying canons of usage, one should also recognize, of course, the far-reaching utility involved. He should realize that he must respect principles of usage in order to move effectively in any circle where correct language is a requisite. In the business world, for instance, he must be able to state his thoughts in such a manner that he will never be misinterpreted. Hence he cannot write such a sentence as

Mr. Stone told Mr. Keane that he must leave.

because the sentence is ambiguous. Instead, he must write

Mr. Stone told Mr. Keane, "I must leave."

or

Mr. Stone told Mr. Keane, "You must leave."

or he must employ other phraseology that will create only one meaning —the meaning he has in mind.

Similarly, in any social or other circle where acceptable usage is demanded, one may not say

He don't know no better.

or

I ain't got no more powder.

or any similar usage that deviates from accepted practice because, rightly or wrongly, these circles invoke language requirements that must be met.

Finally, one should realize that rules for usage are necessary to maintain the uniformity of meaning that language has had across the years. If everyone were suddenly permitted to speak and write as he pleased, a chaotic situation would soon result. Men would not be able to construct legal systems, to write contracts, and to engage in the numerous other activities within society that demand a clear, precise, and uniform expression. Guidelines for usage, therefore, are actually one of society's most important safeguards.

In using this book, the reader can consult the table of contents or the index. The table of contents shows the grouping of material according to subject. The index, naturally, is the customary alphabetical listing of material according to title. In order to facilitate the locating of material, the index has been extensively cross-referenced.

To the many teachers of English on all levels who have given so generously of their time and counsel in the preparation of this book, the author expresses his sincere thanks.

T. E. B.

Contents

The
Most Common Mistakes
in
English Usage

1

Commonly Confused Words

Among the most common errors in usage are those which arise from confusing certain pairs or sets of words. Speakers and writers use these words incorrectly because they have not learned their precise meaning. The following words are among the ones most likely to present difficulty.

1. *Able—capable*

The word "able" means "having the ability to perform a given act." For example,

I am *able* to walk through that swamp.

The word "capable" means (1) "having adequate capacity to do or to make" or (2) "having adequate capacity to receive an action." For example,

He is a *capable* leader.
This book is *capable* of being translated.

A common error arises from the attempt to use "able" for "capable" in the second meaning listed above, i.e., situations in which the "capacity to receive an action" is involved.

Wrong: This law is *able* to be evaded. (Wrong because the capacity to receive an action is involved.)
Right: This law is *capable* of being evaded.
Wrong: This tanker is *able* to be restored.
Right: This tanker is *capable* of being restored.

2. *Accept—except*

"Accept," which is always a verb, means "to receive." For example,

> I *accept* your apology.

"Except" may be either a preposition or a verb. As a preposition, it is used as follows:

> Every boy is here *except* Henry.

As a verb, the word "except" means to "make an exception of." For example,

> We *except* Jimmy from the responsibility.

If one realizes the meaning involved, he should never experience difficulty in knowing which word to use.

Wrong: I shall *except* the gift when he brings it.
Right: I shall *accept* the gift when he brings it.
Wrong: They *excepted* the offer as soon as it was made.
Right: They *accepted* the offer as soon as it was made.
Right: The lawyers *excepted* certain clauses from the agreement.

3. *All ready—already*

The words "all ready" mean that "everything is in readiness" or "everyone is ready."

The word "already" is an adverb which emphasizes the idea that an action is complete at the present moment or was completed at a moment in the past. For example,

> Marian is tired *already*.
> Louis *already* had finished the painting.

Wrong: He is *all ready* five pounds overweight.
Right: He is *already* five pounds overweight.
Wrong: We are *already* for the dance.
Right: We are *all ready* for the dance.
Wrong: The *all ready* heavy load became heavier.
Right: The *already* heavy load became heavier.

4. *All right—alright*

The term "all right" is correct; the word "alright" is non-existent in acceptable usage.

Wrong: Everything was *alright.*
Right: Everything was *all right.*
Wrong: "*Alright*," said he, "that's the end."
Right: "*All right*," said he, "that's the end."

5. *All together—altogether*

The words "all together" have the meaning of "everyone in or at the same location." The word "altogether" means "entirely."

Wrong: We were *altogether* for the first family reunion in ten years.
Right: We were *all together* for the first family reunion in ten years.
Wrong: They were *all together* mistaken in their conclusion.
Right: They were *altogether* mistaken in their conclusion.

6. *Allusion—delusion—illusion*

Using these three words correctly is simply a matter of understanding the definition of each.

The word "allusion" means a "reference." It is the noun form of the verb "allude." For example,

His *allusion* to the national debt was rather pointed.

The word "delusion," defined broadly, is a "fixed abberation of the mind." For example,

The patient suffered from the *delusion* that he was a king.

The word "illusion" means a "situation wherein a person has misinterpreted the data of his senses," or, stated more broadly, he has made an "error in vision or mental perception." For example,

Jean thought she saw a ship on the horizon, but it was an *illusion.*

Wrong: The music created the *delusion* that it was coming from the next room.
Right: The music created the *illusion* that it was coming from the next room.

Wrong: The large furniture on the stage made Marianne appear small, thereby creating a *delusion.*

Right: The large furniture on the stage made Marianne appear small, thereby creating an *illusion.*

Wrong: Mr. Potterby suffered from the *illusion* that he was an executive.

Right: Mr. Potterby suffered from the *delusion* that he was an executive.

Wrong: Mr. Jenning's *illusion* was a belief that he was very seriously ill.

Right: Mr. Jenning's *delusion* was a belief that he was very seriously ill.

Wrong: His *illusion* to my failure was clear.

Right: His *allusion* to my failure was clear.

7. *Alumna—alumnae—alumnus—alumni*

An alumna is a female graduate. Its plural is "alumnae." An alumnus is a male graduate. Its plural is "alumni." In instances involving both sexes, the term "alumni" is used. (Check your dictionary for correct pronunciations.)

Although there has been a tendency in recent years to use the masculine terms for all situations, formal language still requires that the distinction be made.

Wrong: Mary was an *alumnus* of Reed.

Right: Mary was an *alumna* of Reed.

Wrong: The Skidmore (an all-girls' college) *alumni* held a rally.

Right: The Skidmore *alumnae* held a rally.

8. *Amount—number*

The word "amount" is used to denote quantity; the word "number" is used when the objects involved can be counted.

Wrong: The *amount* of horses on the range was small.

Right: The *number* of horses on the range was small.

Wrong: We had a large *amount* of students on hand for the rally.

Right: We had a large *number* of students on hand for the rally.

Right: There was a small *amount* of sugar in the bowl.

Right: The *amount* of money needed became larger every day.

9. *Anxious—eager*

The word "anxious" should be used only when anxiety is involved; it should not be used as a synonym for "eager." The word "eager" means "highly desirous."

Wrong: I am *anxious* to taste the new flavors of ice cream. (Wrong because no anxiety is involved.)
Right: I am *eager* to taste the new flavors of ice cream.
Right: I was *anxious* when my child was thrown from the horse. (Right because anxiety is involved.)

10. *Apt—liable—likely*

Although informal usage permits the synonymous use of the words, "apt," "liable," and "likely," formal usage recognizes a precise use for each.

"Apt" means "has an aptitude for." Hence, a pupil is said to be apt.
"Liable" means "subject to" or "answerable to or for." Hence, a lawbreaker is liable to arrest and the consequences thereof.
"Likely" means "a high degree of probability." Hence, a driver who operates his car recklessly is likely to become involved in an accident.

Wrong: In April, we are *liable* to have rain often.
Right: In April, we are *likely* to have rain often.
Wrong: If the lion is annoyed, he is *apt* to become angry.
Right: If the lion is annoyed, he is *likely* to become angry.
Right: Driving while intoxicated makes one *liable* to fine and imprisonment.

11. *Aware—conscious*

The word "aware" means to "have a cognizance of." For example,

I am *aware* of a feeling of uneasiness in the group.

The word "conscious," basically, pertains to one's physical and mental situation at a given moment. For example,

The injured workman is now *conscious*.

Although the synonymous use of these words is not regarded by editors of dictionaries and other authorities as a serious error, careful speakers and writers should note, nonetheless, the distinction in use.

Informal: I am *conscious* of resentment in that situation.
Formal: I am *aware* of resentment in that situation.
Informal: The President was not *conscious* of a growing opposition.
Formal: The President was not *aware* of a growing opposition.

12. Awful—awfully

The word "awful" is an adjective meaning, in its true sense, "awe inspiring." The adverbial form is "awfully." In a loose sense, these words are used synonymously with such words as "very," "great," "strong," and "powerful."

In formal writing and speaking, of course, these words should not be used loosely. However, when they are used, either formally or loosely, they should be used in their proper (adjective and adverbial) forms.

Wrong: We had an *awful* good time. (Wrong because an adverb is needed to modify the adjective "good.")
Right: We had an *awfully* good time.
Wrong: The owner of the car became *awful* excited.
Right: The owner of the car became *awfully* excited.
Wrong: The stale bread was *awful* hard.
Right: The stale bread was *awfully* hard.

Note: The above instances represent colloquial usage. Below, the formal usage is illustrated.

Right: The appearance of the giant was truly *awful*.
Right: The leader spoke *awfully* of the consequences.

13. Balance—remainder

The word "balance" can be used synonymously with "remainder" only when one is speaking of financial transactions or the keeping of records.

Wrong: We plan to keep the car for the *balance* of the year.
Right: We plan to keep the car for the *remainder* (or rest) of the year.
Wrong: For the *balance* of his vacation, he fished and rested.
Right: For the *remainder* of his vacation, he fished and rested.
Right: His checking account had a *balance* of $426.17.
Right: Our records show a cash *balance* of $2817.39.

14. *Between—among*

One should use the word "between" only when *two* persons, objects, or ideas are under consideration. If *three* or more are involved, he should use the word "among."

Wrong: Between Joe, Pete, and Herb, the controversy was finally settled.
    (Between is wrong because three persons are involved.)
Right: Among Joe, Pete, and Herb, the controversy was finally settled.
Wrong: The matter was to be discussed *between* the electricians, the plumbers, and the carpenters.
Right: The matter was to be settled *among* the electricians, the plumbers, and the carpenters.

15. *Bring—take*

The word "bring" should be used in situations where something is being moved toward the speaker. For example,

    Bring me that book.

The word "take" should be used in situations where something is being moved away from the area of the speaker. For example,

    Take that book with you.

Wrong: I don't know what I should *bring* to the seashore when I leave for my vacation.
Right: I don't know what I should *take* to the seashore when I leave for my vacation.
Wrong: He should *bring* his lunch with him when he leaves for school.
Right: He should *take* his lunch with him when he leaves for school.

16. *Can—may*

The word "can" means "having the ability." The word "may" means "being permitted."

Wrong: Mother says that I *can* go to the party. (Wrong if this situation involves permission.)
Right: Mother says that I *may* go to the party.
Wrong: I shall ask the boss if I *can* have the afternoon off.
Right: I shall ask the boss if I *may* have the afternoon off.

Right: Father says that Johnny *can* drive the car now. (Right if Father is stating that Johnny has the ability.)

Right: Father says that Johnny *may* drive the car now. (Right if Father is stating that Johnny is being granted permission.)

17. *Cannot—can not*

An authoritative ruling has now been established concerning the use of "can not" and "cannot." The correct form is now almost universally considered to be the single word "cannot."

Wrong: I *can not* attend the meeting.
Right: I *cannot* attend the meeting.

18. *Certain—sure*

The words "certain" and "sure" are adjectives; the words "certainly" and "surely" are adverbs. (For a definition of the adjective, see page 68; for a definition of the adverb, see page 68.)

Wrong: I *sure* am tired. (Wrong because an adverb is needed to modify the predicate adjective "tired.")
Right: I *surely* (or *certainly*) am tired.
Right: He is a *sure* (or *certain*) winner in the fourth race.
Right: He is *sure* (or *certain*) to be the winner.

19. *Complected—complexioned*

The word "complected" is accepted, at best, as a colloquialism. The word "complexioned" is, therefore, the correct form.

Wrong: He was a dark-*complected* man.
Right: He was a dark-*complexioned* man.
Wrong: There were many light-*complected* Swedes present.
Right: There were many light-*complexioned* Swedes present.

20. *Continual—continuous*

"Continual" means "with occasional interruption." "Continuous" means "without interruption."

Wrong: The child *continuously* disturbed the class.
Right: The child *continually* disturbed the class.

Wrong: The machine ran *continually* for eight days. (Wrong if there was no interruption.)
Right: The machine ran *continuously* for eight days.

21. *Data—datum*

To avoid confusion in the use of the word "data," one need only remember that when it is used synonymously with "facts" it is plural; when it is used synonymously with "information," it is singular.

The word "datum" (meaning "fact") is, of course, the singular form of the word "data" (facts).

Wrong: The *data* (facts) *is* incorrect.
Right: The *data* (facts) *are* incorrect.
Wrong: The *data* (information) *are* certainly interesting.
Right: The *data* (information) *is* certainly interesting.
Right: This *datum is* subject to challenge.

22. *Disinterested—uninterested*

The term "disinterested" means "not influenced by personal or self-interest." The word "uninterested" means "not interested."

Wrong: I was *disinterested* in the story. (Wrong if the speaker means he was not interested.)
Right: I was *uninterested* in the story.
Wrong: I am an *uninterested* party in the case. (Wrong if the speaker means that he has no self-interest in the case.)
Right: I am a *disinterested* party in the case.

23. *Each other—one another*

In formal English, the expression "each other" is used when *two* persons are involved; and the expression "one another" is used when *three* or *more* persons are involved.

Questionable: The six students were conversing excitedly with *each other*.
Better: The six students were conversing excitedly with *one another*.
Questionable: The couple spoke to *one another* earnestly.
Better: The couple spoke to *each other* earnestly.

24. Enthuse—enthusiastic

The word "enthuse" represents, at best, highly questionable usage. Careful speakers and writers do not use it. The word "enthusiastic" is, of course, the accepted form.

Wrong: We were *enthused* about the idea.
Right: We were *enthusiastic* about the idea.
Wrong: This idea does not make me *enthused*.
Right: This idea does not make me *enthusiastic*.

25. Farther—further

Although many authorities do not consider the interchange of the words "farther" and "further" a serious error, a distinction has long existed between their uses.

The word "farther" should be used in speaking and writing of physical distance, i.e., situations in which distances can be measured. The word "further" should be used in speaking or writing of matters wherein physical measurement is not possible.

Wrong: We walked *further* down the street.
Right: We walked *farther* down the street.
Wrong: We considered the matter *farther*.
Right: We considered the matter *further*.

26. Fewer—less

The word "fewer" should be used only when an actual count can be made. The word "less" should be used when referring to quantity.

Wrong: We have *less* staff members than we had last year.
Right: We have *fewer* staff members than we had last year.
Wrong: They made *less* mistakes with the new calculating machine.
Right: They made *fewer* mistakes with the new calculating machine.
Right: We have *less* trouble now than we had before.

27. Former—latter

If the terms "former" and "latter" are to be used, only two persons or objects may be under consideration. If more than two are involved, these words may not be used.

Wrong: When we consider New York, Chicago, and Los Angeles, the *former* stands out in our minds.

Right: When we consider New York, Chicago, and Los Angeles, the *first named* stands out in our minds.

Wrong: When I think of Paster, Hines, and Clarke, the *latter* seems to be the logical choice.

Right: When I think of Paster, Hines, and Clarke, the *last named* seems to be the logical choice.

Note: Some prominent grammarians question the use of the terms "former" and "latter" to refer to position, as, for example, these terms are used in the sentences above. They contend that "former" and "latter" should be used only to establish a time relationship. For example,

> The *former* president interpreted his duties narrowly.
>
> The *latter* president held strictly to protocol.

28. *Imply—infer*

The words "imply" and "infer" should not be used synonymously. "Imply" should be used by speakers and writers; "infer" should be used by listeners and readers.

Wrong: The lecturer said, "I do not mean to *infer* that I am dissatisfied.

Right: The lecturer said, "I do not mean to *imply* that I am dissatisfied.

Wrong: The audience *implied* that the speaker was a Republican.

Right: The audience *inferred* that the speaker was a Republican.

29. *Lay—lie*

Understanding the uses of the verbs "lay" and "lie" rests on an understanding of the difference between a "transitive verb" and an "intransitive verb."

A *transitive* verb is one which *takes* an object; i.e., the action of the verb carries over to an object. For example,

> He *moved* the table. ("moved" is transitive because it takes an object—"table")

An *intransitive* verb is one which does not take an object; i.e., the action of the verb does not carry over to an object because the intransitive verb never takes an object. For example, the verb in the following sentence is intransitive:

> The sun *rises* early.

Before using any form of the verbs "lay" or "lie," one must remember two facts: (1) the verb "lay" is transitive (i.e., takes an object), while the verb "lie" is intransitive (i.e., does not take an object); (2) the principal parts of "lay" are lay (present), laid (past), laid (past participle), and laying (present participle); while the principal parts of "lie" are lie (present), lay (past), lain (past participle), and lying (present participle).

Wrong: Yesterday I *laid* in bed until noon. (Wrong because the past tense of the verb "lie" is needed because the verb is intransitive.)
Right: Yesterday I *lay* in bed until noon.
Wrong: Last Tuesday I *lay* my hand on the desk. (Wrong because the past tense of the transitive verb "lay" is needed.)
Right: Last Tuesday I *laid* my hand on the desk.
Wrong: He was *laying* in the sun.
Right: He was *lying* in the sun.
Wrong: Now I *lie* me down to sleep.
Right: Now I *lay* me down to sleep. (The object is the pronoun "me.")

30. *Learn—teach*

When one is the receiver of facts or any other type of lesson, he is learning. When he is imparting the information to a second person, he is teaching. Obviously these terms should not be confused.

Wrong: We shall have to *learn* that child to be respectful.
Right: We shall have to *teach* that child to be respectful.
Right: That child must *learn* to be respectful.

31. *Lend—loan*

If one is to be completely formal in his use of language, he must use "lend" as a verb and "loan" as a noun. For example,

> I shall *lend* him $500.
> I shall make him a *loan* of $500.

Although many authorities now sanction the use of "loan" as a verb when referring to financial transactions, one should avoid this use if he is to be precise.

Wrong: I am certain that he will *loan* you his lawn mower.
Right: I am certain that he will *lend* you his lawn mower.

32. Loose—lose

The word "loose" means "free, the opposite of tight." The word "lose" means "to suffer a loss."

Wrong: I do not want to *loose* my wallet.
Right: I do not want to *lose* my wallet.
Right: If we *loosen* the clamps too much, we may *lose* the outboard motor because the vibrations may shake it free.

33. Majority—plurality

The term "majority" means at least one more than half. The word "plurality" means the highest number within a greater number. For example, if 100 members of a club vote in an election which has three candidates, one of them must receive at least 51 votes to have a majority. If none of the candidates receives 51 votes, none has a majority. In such a situation, the candidate receiving the highest number of votes is said to have a "plurality." Thus if A receives 46 votes, B receives 42, and C receives 12, A has received the plurality.

Wrong: President Kennedy was elected by the *majority* of the American voters. (Wrong because President Kennedy did not receive at least 51% of the popular vote.)
Right: President Kennedy was elected by a *plurality* vote.
Wrong: Parker was elected captain because he received 17 of the squad's 36 votes. Therefore, he had the *majority* vote.
Right: Parker was elected captain because he received 17 of the squad's 36 votes. Therefore, he received the *plurality* vote.

34. May—might

The word "may" is often confused with the word "can" (for a discussion of this situation see "Can—may, page 7); and it is also frequently confused with the word "might."

In addition to the meaning of permission which is discussed under "Can—may," the word "may" also has the meaning of "future possibility." For example,

> I *may* be finished tomorrow.
>
> The cold weather *may* remain for a month.

The word "might," on the other hand, has the meaning of a future condition that is dependent upon a hypothesis. (A hypothesis is an assumption made as the basis for another thought.) For example,

> If he would help, I *might* help, too.
>
> If everyone would cooperate, Miller *might* be more lenient.

Notice that each use of "might" is based on a hypothesis which is clearly stated. Sometimes, however, the hypothesis is not stated; it is understood, as is the case in the following sentences:

> This wire *might* hold. (The hypothesis "if you would try it" is understood.)
>
> He *might* do this work well. (The hypothesis "if we were to give him the opportunity" is understood.)

Confusion of the words "may" and "might" can be avoided, therefore, if the speaker or writer examines closely the basic meaning of the thought to be expressed.

Wrong: When it rains, he *might* not want to paint.
Right: When it rains, he *may* not want to paint.
Wrong: I *might* go to New York today.
Right: I *may* go to New York today.
Wrong: This *might* be the end of the line. (No hypothesis is understood.)
Right: This *may* be the end of the line.

35. *Memoranda—memorandum*

"Memoranda" is the plural form of the word "memorandum." Hence, it requires a plural verb. Also worthy of note, however, is the fact that "memorandums" is now acceptable as a synonym for "memoranda." In the most formal of writing, however, "memoranda" is still preferable.

Wrong: The memoranda *is* on the table.
Right: The memoranda *are* on the table.

36. *Moral—morale*

As a noun, "moral" means "a lesson." For example,

The moral is "Don't put all your eggs in one basket."

As an adjective, "moral" means "good or characterized by that which is right." For example,

"Our president is a moral man."

"Morale" means "mental condition, general spirit, frame of mind."

Wrong: The story has no *morale*.
Right: The story has no *moral*.
Wrong: His *morales* are questionable.
Right: His *morals* are questionable.

37. *Party—person*

The word "party" is permissible as a substitute for the word "person" only in legal usage, e.g., "party of the first part." In other writing, one must be careful not to interchange these words.

Wrong: The first *party* I spoke with gave me no encouragement.
Right: The first *person* I spoke with gave me no encouragement.
Wrong: A certain *party* told me that Cliff voted for Jake.
Right: A certain *person* told me that Cliff voted for Jake.

38. *Practicable—practical*

The word "practicable" means "that which appears to be capable of being put into practice; that which appears to be capable of being done." For example,

His plan, I feel certain, is *practicable*.

The word "practical" means that something is "known to be workable or effective." For example,

We were given a *practical* plan for consideration.

Wrong: The senator believes that his plan, which has never been tried in any form, is *practical*.
Right: The senator believes that his plan, which has never been tried in any form, is *practicable*.

Note: The word "practicable" may never be applied to persons. The word "practical," when applied to persons, means "realistic," "calculating," "interested in actual conditions rather than in unknown or untried practices."

Right: Mr. Montour is a *practical* business man.
Right: Our approach to our tax problems must be *practical.*

39. *Precede—proceed*

The confusion between the use of "precede" and "proceed" can be eliminated by learning the basic meaning of each term. The word "precede" means "to go before." For example,

Professors will *precede* associate professors in the procession.

The word "proceed" means "to move forward." For example,

We shall *proceed* with the agenda as we have planned.

Wrong: Joe will *proceed* Jim in the line because he is taller.
Right: Joe will *precede* Jim in the line because he is taller.
Wrong: The month *proceeding* June was, of course, May.
Right: The month *preceding* June was, of course, May.

40. *Principal—principle*

The word "principal" used as a noun means the "head of a school, a main participant, a sum of money invested." Examples are:

The *principal* of the Harris School was there.
He is the *principal* in the crime.
His *principal* was $12,000.

As an adjective, "principal" means "main or most important." For example,

Our *principal* aim is personal satisfaction.

The word "principle" is a noun. It means "a rule, a law, an underlying tenet, an idea that is part of a code of behavior." Examples are:

Courtesy is a *principle* of diplomacy.
Honesty and altruism are two of his most noticeable *principles.*

Wrong: My *principle* objection is that I am tired.
Right: My *principal* objection is that I am tired.
Wrong: I objected to the law on *principal.*
Right: I objected to the law on *principle.*

41. *Prophecy—prophesy*

The word "prophecy" is a noun; the word "prophesy" is a verb

Wrong: My *prophesy* is that he will succeed.
Right: My *prophecy* is that he will succeed.
Wrong: I *prophecy* that he will succeed.
Right: I *prophesy* that he will succeed.

42. *Proved—proven*

The word "proved" is always either a verb or part of a verb phrase. For example:

> Joe *proved* the problem.
> Joe *has proved* the problem.

The word "proven" must always be used as an adjective. For example:

> The salve was a *proven* remedy.
> The problem was *proven.* (In this sentence, "proven" is a past participle serving as a predicate adjective.)

Wrong: He has *proven* the answer by checking. (Wrong because "proven" is serving as part of the verb.)
Right: He has *proved* the answer by checking.
Wrong: It was a *proved* answer to the problem.
Right: It was a *proven* answer to the problem.

43. *Provided—providing*

"Provided" is the past participle of the verb "provide"; it is also a conjunction meaning "if."

"Providing" is the present participle of the verb "provide."

A common error arises with the use of "providing" for "provided" as a conjunction.

Wrong: We shall leave, *providing* that the weather is good. (Wrong because the present participle "providing" cannot be used for the conjunction "provided.")

Right: We shall leave early, *provided* that the weather is good.

Wrong: Providing that he is not tired, he will address the group.

Right: Provided that he is not tired, he will address the group.

Right: Mr. Smathers *was providing* for his future.

Right: Providing for his future, Mr. Smathers saved money at every turn.

44. Raise—rear

In formal writing and speaking, the word "raise" should not be used when referring to the upbringing of one's family. However, "raise" is used when speaking of other forms of life (plants, animals, etc.).

Wrong: We *raised* our children in Topeka, Kansas.

Right: We *reared* our children in Topeka, Kansas.

Wrong: The kennel owner specializes in *rearing* Chihuahuas.

Right: The kennel owner specializes in *raising* Chihuahuas.

45. Raise—rise

The distinction between the use of "raise" and "rise" is simple if one remembers that the verb "raise" takes an object (i.e., is a transitive verb), while the verb "rise" does not take an object (i.e., is an intransitive verb).

The principal parts of "raise" are

raise (present)—*raised* (past)—*raised* (past participle)—*raising* (present participle)

The principal parts of "rise" are

rise (present)—*rose* (past)—*risen* (past participle)—*rising* (present participle)

Wrong: We *rose* the beam above the roof. (Wrong because a transitive verb is needed.)

Right: We *raised* the beam above the roof.

Wrong: The bread was *raising* slowly.

Right: The bread was *rising* slowly.

Note: The use of the verb "arise" follows the pattern of the verb "rise." The following are examples:

We shall *arise* tomorrow at seven o'clock.

John has already *arisen.*

46. *Shall—will*

The distinction between the use of "shall" and "will" is now restricted to formal usage. The rule is as follows: for simple futurity, use "shall" with the first person and "will" with the second and third persons. The term "simple futurity" means a situation that does not involve determination or promise; that is to say, something that will occur in the normal course of events.

Hence, for simple futurity, the forms are

I shall	we shall
you will	you will
he will	they will

For determination or promise, the order is reversed. Hence the forms for determination or promise are

I will	we will
you shall	you shall
he shall	they shall

Wrong: I *will* see him tomorrow because we both take the 8:15 train. (Wrong because no determination or promise is involved. Hence the simple future form should be used.)

Right: I *shall* see him tomorrow because we both take the 8:15 train.

Wrong: He *will* go to school today, whether he wants to go or not. (Wrong because determination is involved.)

Right: He *shall* go to school, whether he wants to go or not.

47. *Should—would*

The words "should" and "would" follow the basic pattern of "shall" and "will" except for the situations noted later.

Wrong: I *would* like to have more coffee. (Wrong because nothing more than simple futurity is implied.)

Right: I *should* like to have more coffee.
Wrong: Joe *should* like another helping of ice cream.
Right: Joe *would* like another helping of ice cream.

Note: There are two additional situations involving the use of "should" and "would" which must be mastered by careful speakers and writers. They are (1) the conditional mood and (2) the obligatory mood.

The conditional mood, as the name implies, involves a situation based on a hypothesis. (This situation is also discussed under "Subjunctive Mood" on page 65.) Examples of the conditional are:

If I were he, I *should* not leave.

If Mary were here, he *would* be more polite.

The obligatory covers the situation wherein one has a duty or an obligation. The obligatory always employs the word "should."

I *should* visit my brother.

Mr. Smith *should* shovel the snow.

We *should* do the work immediately.

48. *Sick—disgusted*

The word "sick" should not be used broadly as a synonym for "displeased," "bored," or similar words. Although its meaning is invariably clear in such instances, it lacks the pointedness needed for precise expression.

Vague: I am *sick* of all this paper work.
Better: I have *grown to dislike* all this paper work.
Vague: We are *sick* of his failures.
Better: We are *displeased* with his failures.

49. *Set—sit*

The verb "set" is transitive (i.e., takes an object). The principal parts of "set" are

set (present)—*set* (past)—*set* (past participle)—*setting* (present participle)

The verb "sit" is intransitive (i.e., does not take an object). The principal parts of "sit" are *sit* (present)—*sat* (past)—*sat* (past participle)—*sitting* (present participle)

Failure to recognize and use the correct forms of these verbs causes many errors in usage.

Wrong: When he came in, he *set* down on the big sofa. (Wrong because an intransitive verb is needed.)
Right: When he came in, he *sat* down on the big sofa.
Wrong: There was Mrs. Hogan *setting* behind the counter.
Right: There was Mrs. Hogan *sitting* behind the counter.
Wrong: He *sat* his plane down in the farmer's pasture. (Wrong because **a** transitive verb is needed.)
Right: He *set* his plane down in the farmer's pasture.

Note: There are some idiomatic and dialectal uses of these verbs which must be recognized. The following forms are all considered correct.

> The sun *sets* today at 7:28.
> We counted nine *setting* hens.
> The table is *set* for two.
> The captain's mind is *set*.

50. *Somewhere—somewheres*

The use of the word "somewheres" is to be condemned on the simple ground that authorities do not sanction its use.

Wrong: We heard a sound *somewheres* in the distant woods.
Right: We heard a sound *somewhere* in the distant woods.
Wrong: Somewheres, there must be an answer.
Right: Somewhere, there must be an answer.

Note: The above rule also applies to "nowhere" and "nowheres."

51. *Suspect—suspicion*

The word "suspicion" is a noun. It can never be used for the verb, "suspect."

Wrong: He *suspicioned* that something was amiss.
Right: He *suspected* that something was amiss.
Wrong: I *suspicion* that he is the guilty person.

Right: I *suspect* that he is the guilty person.
Right: My *suspicion* is that he is the guilty person.

Note: There is a growing tendency to use the word "suspect" rather loosely. Although most authorities sanction a fairly wide use of this word, a caution should be sounded, nonetheless.

Questionable: I *suspect* that Mary is quite capable of filling the role.
Better: I *believe* that Mary is quite capable of filling the role.
Questionable: I *suspect* that the gasoline tank must be nearly empty.
Better: I *think* that the gasoline tank must be nearly empty.

52. *Way—ways*

The word "way" is singular; the word "ways" is plural. One must be careful not to use the plural form for the singular.

Wrong: New York is a long *ways* from Winnipeg.
Right: New York is a long *way* from Winnipeg.
Wrong: Any *ways* you look at the question, he is wrong.
Right: Any *way* you look at the question, he is wrong.
Right: There are three *ways* to travel from Huston to Kenton.
Right: A new ship is on the *ways*.

2

Words Commonly Misused

In everyday written and spoken English, certain words are commonly misused. For example, the word "client," in its formal sense, means "one in whose interest a lawyer acts." This word, however, is commonly misused as a synonym for "customer," "sales prospect," and similar terms. This error undoubtedly owes its origin to the ignorance of one person transmitted to thousands of others who have never bothered to check the meaning.

The great difficulty in handling words commonly misused is, of course, that one must first recognize them. This section treats the words which the author, through investigation, has found to be the ones most widely misused.

53. *Adequate*

The word "adequate" means "enough." Therefore, it should not be used to mean "plentiful," "abundant," or "over-supply." Also, it is an absolute adjective, and, as such, it cannot be qualified by a modifier.

Wrong: The number of books was *more adequate* than we had expected.

Right: The number of books was *more nearly adequate* than we had expected. ("more nearly adequate" actually means "closer to being adequate.")

Wrong: The help given us was not *adequate enough* for our purpose.

Right: The help given us was *not adequate* for our purpose.

Right: The assistance which they offered was *less than adequate.*

Right: The papers supplied to us were *more than adequate.*

54. *Alibi*

The word "alibi" means "a formal defense that a man was not at the scene of the crime when the crime was committed." Although it has long been used carelessly as a synonym for "weak excuse," precise usage demands that it be employed only in its legal sense.

Wrong: Johnny gave a poor *alibi* for not doing his homework.
Right: Johnny gave a poor *excuse* for not doing his homework.
Right: The lawyer proved his client's *alibi* that he was in Canton, Ohio, when the New York hotel manager was beaten and robbed in his office.

55. *Alternative*

In formal language, the noun "alternative" means the second of *two* choices. In other words, if "alternative" or the verb "alternate" is to be used, only **two** choices can be involved.

Wrong: We could golf, or we could have the *alternatives* of swimming or fishing. (Wrong because three possibilities are involved.)
Right: We could golf, or we could go swimming or fishing.
Right: We can vote on the question, or we can follow the *alternative* of letting the issue die in committee.
Right: We chose Mr. Hastings as the delegate and Mr. Henderson as the *alternate.*
Wrong: The coach plans to *alternate* Evans, Jackson, and Windstrom at halfback.
Right: The coach plans to *rotate* Evans, Jackson, and Windstrom at halfback.
Right: The coach plans to *alternate* Harshaw and Teller at fullback.

56. *Average*

If one is to be precise, he should not use the word "average" loosely. This word, from a strict standpoint, can be used only in speaking of situations wherein an arithmetical computation can be made. For example, test grades of a class can be "averaged" and an "average grade" established. When one speaks, however, of men, foods, and other situations wherein no arithmetical computation can be made, he should use a more precise term.

Questionable: The *average* man will not vote for a woman for this office.

Better: Most men will not vote for a woman for this office.

Questionable: The *average* dinner in that restaurant is too highly seasoned.

Better: The *customary* dinner in that restaurant is too highly seasoned.

Questionable: The *average* man of thirty years can undergo this exercise.

Better: The *normal* man of thirty years can undergo this exercise.

57. *Climax*

The word "climax" is basically a literary term meaning "the point in a story where the action is resolved into a single, inescapable conclusion." It is more than a mere "turning point" because every story has several turning points.

Precise usage demands that the word "climax" be used in its literary sense rather than loosely to mean a "high point," an "exciting moment," or similar situation.

Wrong: The *climax* of Stephenson's speech came when he dropped his glasses.

Right: The *most amusing part* of Stephenson's speech came when he dropped his glasses.

Wrong: Thomson reached the *climax* of his sales talk by holding the full case up for his prospective customers to examine.

Right: Thomson reached the *high point* of his sales talk by holding the full case up for his prospective customers to examine.

Right: The business organization reached its *climax* when the court formally declared it bankrupt.

Right: The *climax* of Robertson's athletic career came when his right leg was amputated.

58. *Dilemma*

The word "dilemma" means a situation wherein one faces just "two choices, either of which is unsatisfactory or otherwise objectionable." It should not be used loosely as a synonym for "perplexing situation."

Wrong: I was in a *dilemma* about what to have for dinner.

Right: I faced a *problem* about what to have for dinner.

Wrong: Jim's arriving early presented a real *dilemma.*
Right: Jim's arriving early presented an *embarrassing situation.*

59. *Enable*

The word "enable" means "to give ability, to make able." Therefore, this word should be used only when ability is given.

Wrong: The light woodwork *enables* the room to look more attractive.
Right: The light woodwork *makes* the room look more attractive.
Wrong: The bright cover on the magazine *enabled it* to be seen more easily.
Right: The bright cover on the magazine *enabled the person* looking at it to see it more easily.

60. *Essential*

"Essential" means something that is "necessary for the existence of" something else. For example, a piston is an essential part of an internal combustion motor. "Essential" should not be used synonymously with "important," "highly desirable," and similar expressions.

Wrong: For me, meat for dinner is *essential.*
Right: For me, meat for dinner is *important.*
Wrong: His father's happiness is *essential.*
Right: His father's happiness is a *highly important* consideration.

Note: "Essential" is an absolute adjective. Therefore, one object can never be "more essential" than another.

61. *Extra*

The word "extra" is an adjective meaning "something in addition to that which is due; something beyond that which is expected; something outside of." Examples of the word "extra" used correctly follow:

He gave *extra* time to the project.

We have an *extra* tire in the garage.

Swimming is an *extra*-curricular activity.

A common error arises with the attempt to make the word "extra" an adverb meaning "unusually" or "very."

Wrong: The new ice cream tasted *extra* good.
Right: The new ice cream tasted *very* (or *unusually*) good.

Wrong: The high jumper put forth an *extra* strong effort.
Right: The high jumper put forth an *unusually* strong effort.

62. *Farce*

The word "farce" has two precise meanings. The first, which is now almost obsolete, is "to stuff heavily" as "to place too much within a book." The second is "a work of a humorous nature wherein the emphasis is on the situation rather than on the structure of the work," as in Shakespeare's *A Comedy of Errors.*

In recent years, however, the word has been used very broadly and very loosely to mean something that is characterized by "mockery, sham, hypocrisy, or emptiness." Because this last meaning is so broad, careful speakers and writers should avoid it.

Poor: The procedure for voting was really a *farce.*
Better: The procedure for voting was *characterized* by *dishonesty.*
Poor: They made a *farce* of Hamlet.
Better: Their portrayal of Hamlet was definitely *weak.*

63. *Fix*

The word "fix" must be used with care because of its wide range of meanings. In its precise sense, the word means "to make fast," as

The bracket was *fixed* to the wall.

In its colloquial sense, it ranges from its use as a noun to signify a "predicament" to its use as a verb to mean "to connive or bring to pass in an illegal manner."

Colloquial: We are going to *fix* the broken machine.
Precise: We are going to *repair* the broken machine.
Colloquial: When we lost our oars, we were really in a *fix.*
Precise: When we lost our oars, we were really in a *predicament.*
Colloquial: The politician promised to *fix* the traffic ticket for the grocer.
Precise: The politician promised to *save* the grocer from having to pay the fine stated on the traffic ticket.

64. *Fulsome*

The word "fulsome" is not to be associated with the word "full." "Fulsome" means "offensive, disgusting, or characterized by insincerity."

Wrong: The secretary gave a *fulsome* account of the minutes.
Right: The secretary gave a *full* account of the minutes.
Wrong: It was a *fulsome* occasion. Everyone seemed to be pleased.
Right: It was a *highly pleasant* occasion. Everyone seemed to be pleased.
Right: The outgoing president was given *fulsome* praise. (Right if "insincere" praise is meant. Wrong if "extensive" praise is meant.)

65. *Impeach*

The term "impeach" means to "bring a man to trial with the object of removing him from office if found guilty." It does not mean "to remove from office."

Wrong: No President of the United States has been *impeached.*
Right: One President of the United States, Andrew Johnson, has been impeached.
Right: No President of the United States has been adjudged guilty as a result of impeachment proceeding. Hence, no President of the United States has been removed from office.

66. *Invaluable*

The word "invaluable" is an absolute adjective. Therefore, it cannot be qualified by a modifier.

Wrong: Our cat is *more invaluable* than our dog.
Right: Our cat is *of more value* than our dog.
Wrong: The book will become *more* and *more invaluable* as the years pass.
Right: The book will become *more valuable* as the years pass.
Wrong: That picture is *highly invaluable.*
Right: That picture is *invaluable.*

67. *Livid*

The word "livid" means a "bluish color," "of the color of lead," or the "black and blue coloring of flesh that has received a contusion." This word is commonly used to mean other colors. Also, the word "livid" is absolute and consequently, one object cannot be "more livid" than another.

Wrong: His face was so *livid* that it resembled a red flag.
Right: He was so *enraged* that his face resembled a red flag.
Right: The face of the injured driver was *livid.*

68. *Mutual*

"Mutual" conveys the idea of something that is "reciprocal" or "interchangeable." Although the word is used widely to mean "something held in common," formal usage does not sanction this meaning.

Informal: I met a *mutual* friend of ours yesterday.
Formal: I met a friend of ours yesterday. (Note: The word "common" cannot be substituted for "mutual" because of its connotation.)
Informal: Hubert and Jackson were *mutually* satisfied with the deal.
Formal: Hubert and Jackson were *equally* satisfied with the deal.
Formal: The contract guaranteed the two business establishments *mutual* use of the facilities.

69. *Orphan*

The term "orphan" is commonly used to indicate a person whose mother and father are dead. Actually, only one parent need be deceased in order to term the offspring an "orphan."

Wrong: The boy is not an *orphan* because his father is still living.
Right: The boy is an *orphan*. His mother died four years ago, but his father is still living.

70. *Per*

The word "per" should be used only in standard business expressions, e.g., "percent," "per diem," "per annum." It should not be used synonymously with "in accordance with," "in keeping with," and similar expressions.

Note: Although the word "percent" may be written as one word or two, there is an increasing tendency to write it as a single word.

Wrong: We shall ship the merchandise as *per* your instructions.
Right: We shall ship the merchandise *in accordance with* your instructions.
Wrong: As *per* directions stated, we shall proceed.
Right: *In keeping with* the directions stated, we shall proceed.

71. *Plus*

The word "plus" should not be employed in formal English as a synonym for the conjunction "and."

Wrong: John *plus* four of his friends were on hand.
Right: John *and* four of his friends were on hand.
Wrong: His brashness *plus* his insensitivity made him objectionable.
Right: His brashness *and* his insensitivity made him objectionable.

72. Sadistic

The word "sadistic" refers to a form of sexual perversion. Only careless writers and speakers use it to mean a "strong interest in gory details."

Wrong: Mrs. Jackson's interest in killings stamped her as being *sadistic.*
Right: Mrs. Jackson's interest in killings indicated an *interest* in the *gory aspects* of life.
Right: The psychiatrist was attempting to cure the patient's *sadistic* nature.

73. Unique

The term "unique" means "the only one of its kind." It should not be used to mean "unusual," "strange," "odd." The word "unique" cannot be modified.

Wrong: Mrs. Van der Hof's approach is *unique.* (Wrong unless the fact can be proved that there is no other approach like it.)
Right: Mrs. Van der Hof's approach is *unusual.*
Wrong: Walt Whitman occupies a *most unique* place in literature.
Right: Walt Whitman occupies a *unique* place in literature.

74. Vital

The word "vital," in its basic sense, means "that which is necessary for existence." This word, therefore, should not be used to convey the idea of that which is merely "important" or "highly desirable." It should be used when life or continued existence is involved.

Wrong: Her singing is *vital* to the success of the party. (Wrong unless the party will be an unquestionable failure if she does not sing.)
Right: Her singing *will contribute greatly* to the success of the party.
Right: The importation of rubber is *vital* to our industry.

3

Errors in Using Nouns

Errors in the use of nouns can be classified conveniently under the following headings: (1) errors in agreement with verbs; (2) errors in the use of plurals; (3) errors in case.

This section treats errors in agreement and in plurals; errors in case are treated under a separate heading.

Errors in agreement with verbs can be avoided by determining the noun or pronoun which is the true subject of the verb and then determining whether it is singular or plural. An important rule to remember is:

A verb agrees with its subject in number and in person. If the subject (the noun or the pronoun) is first person singular, the verb must be first person singular. For example,

Jim *is* the secretary. I *am* the chairman.

75. *Determining the Real Subject*

The following sentences illustrate the errors that arise when the true subject of the verb is not determined.

Wrong: A trio of boys *were* scheduled to sing. (Wrong because the subject of the verb is the singular noun "trio.")
Right: A trio of boys *was* scheduled to sing.
Wrong: A box of eggs *are* on the table.
Right: A box of eggs *is* on the table.
Wrong: The memoranda *is* not important. ("memoranda" is plural.)
Right: The memoranda *are* not important.
Wrong: His thoughtlessness and discourtesy *annoys* me.
Right: His thoughtlessness and discourtesy *annoy* me.

Wrong: Joe and Stew *is* to help us.
Right: Joe and Stew *are* to help us.
Wrong: My license *are* in my pocket.
Right: My license *is* in my pocket.
Wrong: The cluster of grapes *are* thick.
Right: The cluster of grapes *is* thick.

76. *Parenthetical Elements—Between Subject and Verb*

Writers and speakers must be especially careful of sentences in which parenthetical elements appear between the subject and the verb because these elements often mislead the writer or the speaker into using a plural verb. Note the following sentence:

John, as well as Jake, *is* responsible for this act.

In this sentence, the verb "is" (a singular form) is used because its subject is "John," which is singular. The phrase "as well as Jake" is a parenthetical element, and consequently has no bearing on the subject.

Wrong: Bayard, with his four fraternity brothers, *are* in the car. (Wrong because the subject of the verb is the noun "Bayard.")
Right: Bayard, with his four fraternity brothers, *is* in the car.
Right: Bayard and his four fraternity brothers *are* in the car. (Note the compound subject in this sentence.)
Wrong: Mr. Philips, together with some friends and neighbors, *are* planning a celebration.
Right: Mr. Philips, together with some friends and neighbors, *is* planning a celebration.

77. *Collective Nouns*

A collective noun, as the name implies, is a noun that represents a collection; that is to say, it is a noun that stands for two or more persons, objects, or ideas.

Generally, collective nouns are regarded as being singular, and consequently they require singular verbs. For example,

The militia *is* quartered in its barracks.

Sometimes, however, they convey a plural idea, and in these instances, they require a plural verb. For example,

The militia *are* discussing the battle among themselves.

Below are illustrated the common errors in agreement that arise with the use of collective nouns as subjects of verbs.

Wrong: The jury *are* giving *their* verdict now. (Wrong because the process of giving a verdict is a collective, hence a singular action.)

Right: The jury *is* giving *its* verdict now.

Wrong: The jury *is* arguing among *itself.* (Wrong because the jury is not arguing collectively. Rather, its members are arguing among themselves.)

Right: The jury *are* arguing among *themselves.*

Wrong: The committee *are* empowered to make a recommendation.

Right: The committee *is* empowered to make a recommendation.

Wrong: The visiting team *are* to defend the west goal.

Right: The visiting team *is* to defend the west goal.

Wrong: Lobster tails *are* the first item on the menu.

Right: Lobster tails *is* the first item on the menu.

78. *Collective Ideas*

Frequently there are situations wherein two or more persons, objects, or ideas which are otherwise singular combine to make a collective thought. For example, in the sentence

Mary and Clarence at the same bridge table *is* unthinkable.

the nouns "Mary" and "Clarence" constitute a collective thought. Hence, the singular verb "is," rather than the plural verb "are," is used.

The important point to be noted is that the collective idea requires a singular verb.

Wrong: Soup and salad *are* too light a lunch. (Wrong because the words "soup and salad" represent a collective idea.)

Right: Soup and salad *is* too light a lunch.

Wrong: A large home and a sizable bank account *are* his aim in life.

Right: A large home and a sizable bank account *is* his aim in life.

Wrong: Hawkins and Thurston *are* a law firm.

Right: Hawkins and Thurston *is* a law firm.

Wrong: Playing the piano and singing simultaneously *are* difficult.

Right: Playing the piano and singing simultaneously *is* difficult.

Wrong: Ham and eggs *are* my favorite breakfast.

Right: Ham and eggs *is* my favorite breakfast.
Wrong: A horse and buggy *were* a necessity in those days.
Right: A horse and buggy *was* a necessity in those days.

79. Subjects Joined by the Conjunction "Or"

When two nouns or pronouns acting as the subjects of a verb are joined by the conjunction "or," the second named noun or pronoun governs the choice of the verb. For example,

> John or I *am* to shovel the snow.
>
> They or we *are* to occupy the first table.
>
> Jane or he *is* to complete the lesson.

The reason for this rule is that the conjunction "or" really makes two sentences. The first sentence above, for instance, actually states

> John is to shovel the snow or I am to shovel the snow.

Wrong: Saunders or I *are* to lead the discussion.
Right: Saunders or I *am* to lead the discussion.
Wrong: Lester or she *are* to call the roll.
Right: Lester or she *is* to call the roll.
Wrong: They or he *are* certain to be called.
Right: They or he *is* certain to be called.

80. Double Subjects

A common error made by children and carried into adult life is the double subject. Below are examples with the corrected form.

Wrong: Bob's brother *he* took the car home.
Right: Bob's *brother* took the car home.
Wrong: Jim and I *we* took the long road.
Right: *Jim* and *I* took the long road.
Wrong: The possum *it* does its hunting at night.
Right: The *possum* does its hunting at night.
Wrong: The Japanese *they* eat a great deal of rice.
Right: The *Japanese* eat a great deal of rice.

Note: The insertion of a comma between the subject and the double subject does not make the use of the double subject correct. For example, the sentences below are incorrect, notwithstanding the use of the comma.

Wrong: The stereotype department, *it* makes the mats.
Right: The stereotype *department* makes the mats.
Wrong: The players, *they* like the idea.
Right: The *players* like the idea.

81. *There is—there are*

The simplest way to keep straight "there is" and "there are" is to remember that any sentence beginning with either of these expressions is inverted. Consequently, before using "there is" or "there are," one should cast the sentence into its natural rather than its inverted order.

The term "natural order" simply means placing the subject before the verb. Note the sentence below as it appears in its inverted order; then examine it in its natural order.

> There are two goldfish in the bowl. (Inverted)
> Two goldfish are there in the bowl. (Natural)

When a sentence of this type is placed in its natural order, one can recognize the subject immediately. Then, of course, he can decide whether the verb is to be singular or plural.

Wrong: There *are* a group ready to enter the room now. (Wrong because the subject is the noun "group.")
Right: There *is* a group ready to enter the room now.
Wrong: There *is* a few points to be made in this argument.
Right: There *are* a few points to be made in this argument.
Wrong: There *goes* old Mrs. Lennox and her meek little husband.
Right: There *go* old Mrs. Lennox and her meek little husband.
Wrong: Here *comes* my brother and his friend.
Right: Here *come* my brother and his friend.

82. *Correlative Conjunctions and Subjects*

A correlative conjunction is one which works in correlation with another conjunction. Examples are: "either . . . or," "neither . . . nor," "as . . . as," "not so . . . as." When nouns or pronouns acting as subjects are used with correlative conjunctions, the choice of the verb is determined by the second noun or pronoun.

Note the following use of correlative conjunctions:

Either Joe or Herm *is* coming.
Neither Albert nor I *am* leaving.

In each of the sentences above, the verb agrees with the second noun or pronoun.

Wrong: Neither Smith nor Martin *are* responsible. (Wrong because the verb must agree with the singular noun "Martin.")
Right: Neither Smith nor Martin *is* responsible.
Wrong: Pete or I *is* responsible for the accident.
Right: Pete or I *am* responsible for the accident.
Wrong: Either Clemson or Tulane *are* represented.
Right: Either Clemson or Tulane *is* represented.

83. *Plural Nouns Commonly Misused as Singulars*

Following is a list of nouns that are always plural. While many of these nouns are commonly misused as singulars by giving them singular verbs, they are plural. Therefore, they require plural verbs.

annals	nuptials	snippers
ashes	oats	spectacles
billiards	obsequies	suds
clothes	pants	thanks
dregs	pliers	thongs
eaves	pincers	tongs
entrails	proceeds	trousers
goods	remains	tweezers
leavings	riches	victuals
lees	scissors	vitals
links	shears	wages

Wrong: My scissors *is* not very sharp.
Right: My scissors *are* not very sharp.
Wrong: His clothes *is* certainly expensive.
Right: His clothes *are* certainly expensive.
Wrong: The courthouse annals *is* not the place to look for the date of the marriage.
Right: The courthouse annals *are* not the place to look for the date of the marriage.

84. *Plural Nouns Considered as Singulars*

One of the most troublesome questions in agreement is that of recognizing the nouns which are always singular, the nouns which are always plural, and the nouns which may be either.

The following words, although plural in form, are generally considered singular in meaning. Hence they nearly always require singular verbs.

acoustics	hydromechanics	phonics
aeronautics	linguistics	physics
alms	magnetics	pneumatics
analytics	mathematics	poetics
athletics	means (wealth	politics
bellows	or way)	rickets
civics	measles	spherics
comics	metaphysics	statics
dynamics	molasses	statistics
economics	mumps	tactics
esthetics	news	United States
ethics	optics	whereabouts
hydraulics	phonetics	

Note: Some of the above words can be plural on rather unusual occasions.

Right: The politics of the three brothers *are* sharply different. (Right because "politics" in this instance means political beliefs.)

Right: The measles which the three children have *are* of different nature and duration. (Right because "measles" is basically plural.)

Right: The acoustics of the two buildings *are* sharply different. (Right because "acoustics" is basically plural.)

Right: The athletics of the college *are* football, basketball, and baseball. (Right because "athletics" in this sentence is used synonymously with "sports activities.")

85. *Singular Forms Replacing Plural Forms*

On some occasions, singular forms replace plural forms when the noun becomes an adjective. Although the singular form is used, the word remains basically plural in meaning. The sentences below illustrate singular forms used as plurals.

Right: The room was fifteen feet wide. Hence it was a fifteen-*foot* room.
Right: We walked three miles. It was, therefore, a three-*mile* walk.
Right: The surgeon made an incision of three inches. It was, therefore, a three-*inch* incision.
Right: The referee penalized the team fifteen yards. The fifteen-*yard* penalty put them against the goal line.
Right: The contractor planned to construct a forty-*house* project.
Right: Mr. Casper is building a three-*car* garage.
Right: Mr. Milton wants a nine-*room* home.
Right: We saw a four-*man* bobsled.

86. *Feminine versus Masculine Forms*

Within the past three decades, there has been a decided tendency to drop feminine forms of nouns in favor of masculine forms for both masculine and feminine. The following are some of the feminine forms of nouns which are rarely used. Instead, the masculine form (listed in parentheses after the feminine form) has become standard for both masculine and feminine.

administratrix (administrator), aviatrix (aviator), benefactress (benefactor), directress (director), editress (editor), executrix (executor), huntress (hunter), inheritrix (inheritor), poetess (poet)

Obsolescent: Edna St. Vincent Millay, an American *poetess*, wrote many fine sonnets.
Current Form: Edna St. Vincent Millay, an American *poet*, wrote many fine sonnets.
Obsolescent: Mrs. Peterson was formerly a *directress* of a girls' school.
Current Form: Mrs. Peterson was formerly a *director* of a girls' school.

Note: In recent years, feminists have striven to influence the matter of feminine versus masculine forms.

In some instances, they have been quite effective in promoting the use of new forms—e.g., "Ms." (to make irrelevant a woman's marital status); "chairperson" (to offset any prejudice inherent in "chairman" and "chairlady"); "six-person" committee.

In other instances, they have had only a limited success—e.g., "gentlepersons" (for "gentlemen"); telephone "repairperson;" "person-in-the-street" opinions.

In still other instances, they have failed rather badly—e.g., "Trust God—She will help you;" "person" the emergency stations; "parent" the ill child.

4

Errors in Using Pronouns

Errors in the use of pronouns can be classified conveniently under the following headings: (1) errors in agreement with verbs; (2) errors arising with the use of antecedents; (3) errors in case; and (4) miscellaneous errors.

The basic rules for agreement of subject and verb which were treated in the preceding section on Errors in Nouns (see pages 31-38) should be reviewed because they pertain to pronouns also. Errors in case are covered under a separate heading (see page 49). This section, therefore, treats errors in agreement with verbs that pertain only to pronouns; errors arising with the use of antecedents; and miscellaneous errors.

One of the most important rules to remember regarding errors in agreement of pronouns serving as subjects is the one stated on page 31:

A verb must agree with its subject in number and in person. This rule is very important, for if one can apply it properly, he can avoid some of the most common errors in agreement.

A source of genuine difficulty in handling pronouns lies in the fact that some are always singular; some are always plural; and some may be either singular or plural. The following discussion treats common errors in agreement of pronouns.

87. *Everyone—and Similar Pronouns—Use of*

The pronoun "everyone," which is synonymous with the pronoun "everybody," is always singular. Similarly, the pronouns "someone," "one," "no one," "somebody," "nobody" are singular. In using these pronouns, one must be especially careful to make the verb agree, and he must also make any pronoun substituted for one of them singular.

Wrong: Everyone *were* singing from *their* books as *they* entered the room. (Wrong because the verb and the pronouns substituted for "everyone" do not agree with the singular pronoun "everyone.")

Right: Everyone *was* singing from *his* book as *he* entered the room.

Wrong: Everybody *accept their* responsibilities.

Right: Everybody *accepts his* responsibilities.

Wrong: No one among the players *are* going to want to work hard.

Right: No one among the players *is* going to want to work hard.

Wrong: If anyone *are* going to help, *they* should state *their* intention now.

Right: If anyone *is* going to help, *he* should state *his* intention now.

Wrong: Nobody in that group *have their* reports up to date, as *they* should have.

Right: Nobody in that group *has his* reports up to date, as *he* should have.

88. *Either and Neither—Use of as Pronouns*

The words "either" and "neither" can be correlative conjunctions, adjectives, or pronouns. The following illustrates each use:

Either Mary *or* I am to speak next. (Correlative conjunction)

Either player may be used at halfback. (Adjective)

Neither is a very reliable substitute. (Pronoun)

When "either" or "neither" is used as a pronoun, it is always singular.

Wrong: Either of the boys *are* acceptable to do the errands. (Wrong because the verb should be singular to agree with the subject "either.")

Right: Either of the boys *is* acceptable to do the errands.

Wrong: Neither of the courses *are* acceptable in meeting this requirement for graduation.

Right: Neither of the courses *is* acceptable in meeting this requirement for graduation.

Wrong: I liked the tenor and the soprano, but neither *were* really top flight.

Right: I liked the tenor and the soprano, but neither *was* really top flight.

89. *It—Used as an Indefinite Pronoun*

When the pronoun "it" is used indefinitely, it is singular, even though the noun in the predicate may be plural. (The indefinite "it" is frequently termed an "expletive.")

Wrong: It *are* the freshmen who feel this regulation most keenly.
    (Wrong because the indefinite "it" requires a singular verb.)
Right: It *is* the freshmen who feel this regulation most keenly.
Wrong: It *are* the snowfalls that do the real damage.
Right: It *is* the snowfalls that do the real damage.

90. *Both, Few, Many, Several—Use of as Pronouns*

When the words "both," "few," "many," and "several" are used as pronouns, they are always plural and therefore require plural verbs.

Wrong: Both of the mice *is* underfed.
Right: Both of the mice *are* underfed.
Wrong: Of all the boxes, few *is* left.
Right: Of all the boxes, few *are* left.
Wrong: When you put in the bolts, remember that several *is* required for each support.
Right: When you put in the bolts, remember that several *are* required for each support.

91. *All, Any, None, Some—Use of as Pronouns*

The words "all," "any," "none," "some" used as pronouns may be singular or plural, according to their meaning.

Right: All I have left *is* a few books. ("All" represents, in essence, a collective idea.)
Right: All of the club *are* planning to attend. ("All" represents a plural number of members.)
Right: *Is* any of the cake left?
Right: *Are* any of the boys here?
Right: Of all the veterans, none *is* left.
Right: None of the books *are* here.
Right: Some of the roof *was* torn away from the wall.
Right: Some of them *are* planning a reunion.

92. *One versus You*

The pronoun "one" should be used in the general sense of "anyone" or "everyone."

The pronoun "you" should be used only when addressing a specific person or persons, i.e., second-person use.

Wrong: If *you* live in Florida one day and in Iceland the next, you are certain to feel the change in temperature. (Wrong because this fact is true of anyone having this experience.)

Right: If *one* lives in Florida one day and in Iceland the next, he is certain to feel the change in temperature.

Wrong: *You* must fasten *your* safety belt when the plane is flying through a storm. ("You" is wrong if the speaker means that everyone must fasten his safety belt. If, however, he is addressing an individual who has not fastened his belt, he may use the second person "you.")

Right: *One* must fasten *his* safety belt when the plane is flying through a storm. ("One" is used because this situation is applicable to everyone in the plane. In other words, it is a statement made of everyone, rather than a statement made to a specific person concerning that person only.)

93. *One—Faulty Repetition of*

When the pronoun "one" can be clearly seen as the antecedent, it should not be repeated. Rather, the pronoun "he" should be used.

Wrong: When one is ill, *one* is likely to be impatient.

Right: When one is ill, *he* is likely to be impatient.

Wrong: When one has one's heart set on a goal, *one* is certain to feel disappointment keenly.

Right: When one has his heart set on a goal, *he* is certain to feel disappointment keenly.

94. *He, She—His, Her*

In days gone by, grammarians insisted on an extensive and precise pattern of rules to govern the use of "he" and "she" and "his" and "her." Now, however, the rules have been simplified as follows:

In situations involving only the male sex or in situations involving both the male and the female sexes, the pronouns "he" and "his" are to be used. For example,

> Every man must put *his* gun in place before *he* leaves.
>
> Every student must take *his* book with *him* to his class. (The above sentence may refer to males only or to males and females.)

In situations involving the female sex alone, the practice is now to use feminine pronouns. For example,

> Every student must sign *her* name on *her* roster card.
>
> Each participant is asked to furnish *her* equipment.

95. *Relative Pronoun—Agreement of with Verb*

When a relative pronoun is acting as the subject of a verb, one must be careful to recognize its antecedent (the noun or pronoun to which it refers), because the number and the person of the antecedent determines the number and the person of the verb. For example,

> It is I who *am* the loser. ("Who" is first person singular because its antecedent, "I", is first person singular. Therefore, the verb "am" must agree with "who.")

Below are illustrated the common errors that arise from failure to recognize the antecedent of the relative pronoun.

Wrong: Joe is the one of the boys who *are* on time. (Wrong because the verb must agree with the relative pronoun "who" which is third person singular because its antecedent, "one," is third person singular. Note especially the function of the word "the" in creating the meaning of this sentence.)

Right: Joe is the one of the boys who *is* on time.

Wrong: Joe is one of the boys who *is* on time. (Wrong because in this sentence the antecedent of "who" is "boys." Note that the word "the" does not appear in this sentence.)

Right: Joe is one of the boys who *are* on time.

Wrong: It is I who *is* to make the call.

Right: It is I who *am* to make the call.

Wrong: It was they who *was* to do the work.

Right: It was they who *were* to do the work.

96. *Antecedents—Agreement of Pronouns with*

A pronoun must agree with its antecedent in number, gender, and person. (The term "antecedent" means the noun or the pronoun to which a later pronoun refers.)

Wrong: Every player brought *their* uniform. (Wrong because the antecedent of "their" is "player.")
Right: Every player brought *his* uniform.
Wrong: Everyone was in *their* place when the bell rang.
Right: Everyone was in *his* place when the bell rang.
Wrong: It is I who *is* next. (Wrong because the antecedent of "who" is "I.")
Right: It is I who *am* next.
Wrong: It is you who *is* to choose.
Right: It is you who *are* to choose.

97. *Antecedents—Implied*

Occasionally a pronoun that normally refers to an antecedent may be used without an antecedent. In such instances, the antecedent is implied.

Right: Because every one of the team wanted to play the post-season game, the coach discussed the prospects with *them*. (The antecedent of "them" is not "team"; it is, rather, the word "players," "members," or some similar term that is implied.)
Right: Since only one in the jury responded to the foreman's question, he looked at *them* questioningly.
Right: As the crowd began to assemble in the meeting room, the President began to scan *their* faces.

Note: One must guard against the vague reference treated under heading #99, page 45, when using the implied antecedent.

98. *It's and Its*

Understanding the use of "it's" and "its" is simply a matter of remembering that (1) "it's" is two words—"it" and "is," and (2) "its" is a possessive pronoun.

Wrong: The dog has *it's* bone.
Right: The dog has *its* bone.

Wrong: Its a long way home.
Right: It's a long way home.

99. *That and This—Vague Use of*

The practice of using the relative pronouns "that" and "this" without a concrete antecedent has a tendency to make the sentence vague.

Wrong: Mr. Lewis was always interrupting his wife. *That* annoyed her very much.
Right: Mr. Lewis was always interrupting his wife. *His interruptions* annoyed her very much.
Wrong: Mr. Tompkins always arrives on time, and he works steadily until the final whistle. *This* is very important in the business world.
Right: Mr. Tompkins always arrives on time, and he works steadily until the final whistle. *Punctuality* and *industry* are very important in the business world.

100. *They—Use of in an Indefinite Sense*

The pronoun "they" must not be used carelessly in an indefinite sense—especially when it is not needed. When a pronoun is used without a definite antecedent, it may result in vague reference.

Wrong: In China *they* honor their elderly people more than we honor ours. (Wrong because there is no basis for a clearly implied antecedent.)
Right: The Chinese honor their elderly people more than we honor ours.
Wrong: Our teacher told us that in *France* they eat horsemeat.
Right: Our teacher told us that the *French* eat horsemeat.

101. *Theirselves—Themselves*

The word "theirselves" is not accepted in good usage. The correct form is "themselves."

Wrong: They *theirselves* were on hand for the show.
Right: They *themselves* were on hand for the show.
Wrong: They are hurting *theirselves* by their conduct.
Right: They are hurting *themselves* by their conduct.

102. *Them—Used as a Demonstrative Adjective*

The pronoun "them" may never be used as a demonstrative adjective

Wrong: He put *them* boxes on the shelf.
Right: He put *those* boxes on the shelf.
Wrong: Where are *them* bolts we were using?
Right: Where are *those* bolts we were using?

103. *What—Incorrect Use of*

Although some authorities now accept the pronoun "what" as an all-purpose pronoun, formal English frowns on using it in an instance where it has a clearly stated antecedent. In other words, formal English does not permit "what" to have an antecedent.

Similarly, formal English does not sanction the substitution of "what" for "that which."

Wrong: This is the case *what* I want. (Wrong because "what" has an antecedent, "case.")
Right: This is the case *that* I want.
Informal: In order to eliminate *what* is undesirable, we must censor the story.
Formal: In order to eliminate *that which* is undesirable, we must censor the story.

104. *Which—Loose Use of*

The relative pronoun "which" must not be used in a manner that creates doubt about its antecedent.

Wrong: I shall go bathing today if the water is warm enough *which* I doubt. (Wrong because the pronoun "which" has no definite antecedent.
Right: I shall go bathing today if the water is warm enough. However, I doubt that it will be.
Wrong: We shall drive if the roads are clear *which* I think they are.
Right: We shall drive if the roads are clear *as* I think they are.

105. *Who*

The pronoun "who" is variously termed a "relative" pronoun, an "interrogative" pronoun, and a "personal" pronoun, according to its function in a given instance. The two most important facts to remember about "who" are: (1) it is used only to refer to people; and (2) it is always in the nominative case.

The following errors deal with the failure to use the pronoun "who" only in reference to people.

Wrong: The dog we always feed is the one *who* wags his tail furiously.
Right: The dog we always feed is the one *that* wags his tail furiously.
Wrong: The elephant *who* stands in the first cage is really large.
Right: The elephant *that* stands in the first cage is really large.

The following errors deal with the failure to use the pronoun "who" as a nominative case pronoun. (Nominative case is treated on page 50.)

Wrong: Who did you choose yesterday? (Wrong because the pronoun "who" is being used as the object of the verb "choose.")
Right: Whom did you choose yesterday?
Wrong: Who did you give the book to? (Wrong because the pronoun "who" is being used as the object of the preposition "to.")
Right: Whom did you give the book to?
Wrong: I shall speak to *whomever* is there. (Wrong because the pronoun "whomever" is being used as the subject of the verb "is." In this instance, the object of the preposition "to" is the complete clause, "whoever is there.")
Right: I shall speak to *whoever* is there.
Wrong: I shall accompany the winners, *whomever* they may be. (Wrong because "whomever" cannot be used as a nominative case pronoun.)
Right: I shall accompany the winners, *whoever* they may be.

106. *Whose*

In days past, authorities did not permit the use of the pronoun "whose" in any instance where it did not refer to a person. Now, there is almost no opposition to its use in many instances where its antecedent is an inanimate object.

Acceptable: This is a newspaper *whose* circulation has risen rapidly.
   (The antecedent of "whose" is the inanimate object "newspaper.")
Formal: This is a newspaper the circulation *of which* has risen rapidly.
Acceptable: It was a college *whose* excellence was beyond question.
Formal: It was a college *with* an excellence beyond question.

107. *Whom*

The pronoun "whom," like the pronoun "who" with which it is often confused (see preceding section), is variously a "relative," an "interrogative," and a "personal" pronoun. If one understands the principal reasons for the use of the objective case, he should be able to use the pronoun "whom" correctly.

The following sentences deal with errors in the use of the pronoun "whom." The rules for the use of the objective case are treated on page 51.

Wrong: Who did you see last night in New York? (Wrong because the nominative case pronoun "who" cannot be used as the object of the verb.)

Right: Whom did you see last night in New York?

Wrong: Who do you want to help you? (Wrong because the nominative case pronoun "who" cannot be used as the subject of the infinitive.)

Right: Whom do you want to help you?

Wrong: Who should I give the book to now? (Wrong because the nominative case pronoun "who" cannot be used as the object of a preposition.)

Right: Whom should I give the book to now?

Wrong: Who did the cook give the dinner? (Wrong because the nominative case pronoun "who" cannot be used as an indirect object of a verb, i.e., the object of an understood preposition.)

Right: Whom did the cook give the dinner?

5

Errors in Case

Many errors in usage stem from a lack of knowledge of case. The term "case" actually means the relationship of a noun or a pronoun to another word in the sentence. If, for example, a noun or a pronoun is serving as the subject of a verb, it is said to be in the "nominative case." If it is serving as the object of the verb, it is said to be in the "objective case."

In order to understand case, one should remember three basic facts: (1) every noun and every pronoun is in one of three cases—nominative, objective, possessive; (2) the case of a noun or a pronoun is determined purely by its function; (3) the so-called "rules" for case involve simply the recognition of the function of the noun or the pronoun.

Before one can determine the function of nouns or pronouns, he must learn to divide sentences into elements, for only in this way can he see function clearly. The term "element" means a natural grouping of words—usually the verb and every word related to it. For example, in the following sentence,

It is I who am to work for you.

the elements are "It is I," "who am to work," "for you." Sometimes the grouping of elements may seem unnatural, as in the following sentence:

Whom do you want, may I ask, for this task?

The elements in this sentence are "you do want whom," "I may ask," "for this task."

Establishing the case of a noun or a pronoun can be accomplished in three simple steps: (1) make certain that a given word is a noun or a pronoun; (2) divide the sentence into elements; (3) determine the

49

case of the noun or the pronoun by determining its function in its element.

Nouns present almost no difficulty in English because they do not change their form except in the possessive case. The pronouns, however, can present considerable difficulty if one does not know the pronominal forms for the three cases (nominative, objective, possessive), and if one does not study the rules carefully. After one has mastered these rules, however, they present little difficulty.

The following are the pronouns for the three cases. Following these lists is a discussion of the basic rules for the three cases.

Nominative Case	*Objective Case*	*Possessive Case*
I	me	my
you	you	your
she	her	her
he	him	his
it	it	its
we	us	our
they	them	their
who	whom	whose

108. *Subject of a Verb*

The subject of a verb is always in the nominative case. Hence, if a pronoun is to be used as the subject of a verb, it must be a nominative case pronoun (i.e., it must be one of the pronouns listed above under "Nominative Case"). The following sentences illustrate the noun and the pronoun used as subjects of a verb:

I sing. *John* and *she* are partners. *It* is I *who* am ready.

Wrong: John and *her* were in the front row. (Wrong because a nominative case pronoun, rather than an objective case pronoun, is needed.)

Right: John and *she* were in the front row.

Wrong: Harrison and *me* are the first in line.

Right: Harrison and *I* are the first in line.

Wrong: The Harshaws and *us* are going swimming.

Right: The Harshaws and *we* are going swimming.

Wrong: It is the Robinsons *whom,* I feel certain, are to come.

Right: It is the Robinsons *who,* I feel certain, are to come.
Wrong: Whom, may I ask, should receive the offer?
Right: Who, may I ask, should receive the offer?

109. *Predicate Nominative*

A predicate nominative is a noun or a pronoun which has three characteristics: (1) it is located in the predicate (the part of the sentence from the verb onward); (2) it usually follows a form of the verb "to be" (i.e., "am," "is," "was," "were," "be," "been"); (3) it always renames the subject.

The predicate nominative is also known by the terms "subjective complement" and "predicate noun."

If a pronoun is serving as a predicate nominative, it must be, of course, a nominative case pronoun. The following are examples of the predicate nominative:

It is *I.* That was *John.* This is *she.* That must have been *he.*

Wrong: That was *me* whom you saw yesterday. (Wrong because the objective case pronoun "me" cannot be used as a predicate nominative.)
Right: That was *I* whom you saw yesterday.
Wrong: The leader may be *him,* but I don't think so.
Right: The leader may be *he,* but I don't think so.
Wrong: It was *her* who first saw the intruder.
Right: It was *she* who first saw the intruder.
Wrong: If I were *him,* I should not accept the post.
Right: If I were *he,* I should not accept the post.
Wrong: Whomever it may be, I wish him success.
Right: Whoever it may be, I wish him success.
Wrong: We shall support the president, *whomever* the president may be.
Right: We shall support the president, *whoever* the president may be.

110. *Object of a Verb*

The object of a verb is always in the objective case. Therefore, pronouns used as the object of a verb must be objective case pronouns. The following sentences illustrate the object of a verb:

We painted the *house.* Mr. Masters chose *him.* *Whom* do you want?

Wrong: We chose John and *she* for the committee. (Wrong because the nominative case pronoun "she" cannot be used as the object of a verb.)
Right: We chose John and *her* for the committee.
Wrong: Who do you want?
Right: Whom do you want?
Wrong: The principal put another group and *we* in the same room.
Right: The principal put another group and *us* in the same room.
Wrong: The coach put Jim and *I* on the second team.
Right: The coach put Jim and *me* on the second team.

111. *Object of a Preposition*

A noun or a pronoun serving as the object of a preposition is in the objective case. Hence, pronouns serving as objects of prepositions must be objective case pronouns.

Wrong: Between you and *I,* this should be an easy task. (Wrong because the nominative case pronoun "I" cannot be used as the object of a preposition.)
Right: Between you and *me,* this should be an easy task.
Wrong: The answer looked wrong to Jimmy and *he.*
Right: The answer looked wrong to Jimmy and *him.*
Wrong: Marianne demanded assistance for Marjorie and *she.*
Right: Marianne demanded assistance for Marjorie and *her.*

112. *Indirect Object of the Verb*

The indirect object of the verb is always in the objective case. Therefore, only objective case pronouns may be used to serve as indirect objects of verbs.

An important fact to remember: the indirect object of a verb is always the object of the preposition "to" or the preposition "for" understood.

Wrong: The usher gave Lynn and *he* the aisle seats. (Wrong because the nominative case pronoun "he" cannot be used as the indirect object of the verb.)
Right: The usher gave Lynn and *him* the aisle seats.
Wrong: Please read Paul and *I* that story.
Right: Please read Paul and *me* that story.

Wrong: If you tell Cass and *he* that they are wrong, I think that they will improve.

Right: If you tell Cass and *him* that they are wrong, I think that they will improve.

Wrong: The coach gave *they* and *we* a lecture.

Right: The coach gave *them* and *us* a lecture.

113. *Subject of the Infinitive*

The subject of the infinitive is always in the objective case. Therefore, when pronouns are used as the subjects of infinitives, they must be objective case pronouns.

Note that in the following sentence the pronoun "me" is the subject of the infinitive "to sing"; it is not the object of the verb "ordered."

The conductor ordered *me* to sing.

Wrong: It was I *who* he wanted to come. (Wrong because an objective case pronoun is needed to serve as the subject of the infinitive "to come.")

Right: It was I *whom* he wanted to sing.

Wrong: That was Pete *who* the captain asked to help the corporal.

Right: That was Pete *whom* the captain asked to help the corporal.

Wrong: The teacher told *he* and *I* to leave early.

Right: The teacher told *him* and *me* to leave early.

114. *Case of Nouns and Pronouns Used in Apposition*

If a noun or a pronoun is used in apposition (see page 107 for an explanation of appositives), the noun or the pronoun takes the case of the noun or the pronoun with which it is in apposition.

Wrong: The leaders, Joe and *me,* had a score of 21. (Wrong because "Joe and me" is in apposition to the nominative case noun "leaders.")

Right: The leaders, Joe and *I,* had a score of 21.

Wrong: They chose the old officers, Joe and *she.* (Wrong because "Joe and she" is in apposition to the objective case noun "officers.")

Right: They chose the old officers, Joe and *her.*

Wrong: The winners, Bob and *her,* treated the losers, *they* and *we.*

Right: The winners, Bob and *she,* treated the losers, *them* and *us.*

115. *But—Used as a Preposition*

When the word "but" has the meaning of "except," it becomes a preposition. Therefore, its object (noun or pronoun) falls in the objective case. For example, in the sentence,

Everyone was there *but* me.

the pronoun "me" is in the objective case because it is the object of the preposition "but."

Errors in case that arise when the word "but" is a preposition usually occur when there is a compound (two or more) object, as is shown in the sentences below.

Wrong: The class wanted to criticize everyone but Clem and *I*. (Wrong because the nominative case "I" cannot be used as the object of the preposition "but.")
Right: The class wanted to criticize everyone but Joe and *me*. (Right because the objective case "me" is needed to serve as the object of the preposition.)
Wrong: No seniors but *she* and *he* really wanted the rule.
Right: No seniors but *her* and *him* really wanted the rule.
Wrong: They did not object to anyone but Mary and *he*.
Right: They did not object to anyone but Mary and *him*.

116. *Gerunds—Modified by Possessive*

A "gerund" is the "ing" form of a verb used as a noun, e.g., "running," "swimming," "singing." If the gerund is to be modified by a noun or a pronoun (which really becomes an adjective in this instance), the noun or the pronoun must be in the possessive case if it stands for a person.

This rule can be understood by studying the errors treated below.

Wrong: Father objected to *Mary* singing.
Right: Father objected to *Mary's* singing.
Wrong: Mr. Haskins disliked *me* asking so many questions.
Right: Mr. Haskins disliked *my* asking so many questions.
Wrong: We were not impressed by *him* speaking softly.
Right: We were not impressed by *his* speaking softly.

117. *Gerunds and Participles—Confusion of*

The gerund must not be confused with the present participle (see preceding discussion) because the case of the accompanying noun or pronoun is different in each instance. To avoid mistakes, one must first remember the definition of the gerund and of the participle.

As stated above, the gerund is the "ing" form of the verb used as a *noun*. The present participle, on the other hand, is the "ing" form of the verb used as an *adjective*. Examples of the present participle are:

> The *singing* waiter entered the room. ("singing" modifies the noun "waiter.")
>
> *Singing* merrily, he entered the room. ("singing" modifies the pronoun "he.")

If a gerund is used, the accompanying noun or pronoun must be in the possessive case. If, however, a participle is used, the accompanying noun or pronoun is in either the nominative or the objective case, according to its function. The role of the participle, therefore, is to modify the noun or the pronoun.

Difficulty arises in using the gerund and the participle of certain verbs because either one may often be used logically. Hence, the speaker or writer must exercise care for fear he may create a meaning he does not want. The sentences below illustrate the difference in meaning created as one uses each of these forms.

Right: The teacher saw *me* conversing with Joe. (Right because this sentence says that the teacher saw *me* as I was conversing with Joe. Therefore, a participle is needed to modify the pronoun "me.")

Right: The teacher saw *my* conversing with Joe. (Right because this sentence says that the teacher saw my *act* of conversing with Joe. Therefore, a possessive is needed to modify the gerund "conversing.")

Right: We pictured *him* shouting at the audience. ("shouting" is a participle.)

Right: We pictured *his* shouting at the audience. ("shouting" is a gerund.)

Right: Mother detected *him* eating an apple. ("eating" is a participle. Therefore, mother detected him as a person.)

Right: Mother detected *his* eating an apple. ("eating" is a gerund. Therefore, Mother detected the act.)

118. *Reflexive Pronouns—Errors in Use of*

In formal English, a reflexive pronoun (myself, yourself, himself, etc.) may not be substituted for a nominative or an objective case pronoun.

Wrong: Herman and *myself* were in the prow of the old boat.
Right: Herman and *I* were in the prow of the old boat.
Wrong: She chose Yates and *myself* for the task.
Right: She chose Yates and *me* for the task.

When the subject of the verb is also the receiver of the action, the action is "reflected." Hence, reflexive pronouns may be used to reflect action.

Right: John gives *himself* credit for the promotion.
Right: We labeled *ourselves* "first class."
Right: Father cut *himself* while shaving.

Reflexive pronouns may be used for emphasis:

Right: Henry did the work *himself*.
Right: I shall keep the box *myself*.
Right: They will be on hand *themselves*.

Reflexive pronouns may also be used in certain idiomatic constructions:

Right: I *myself* do not care. (This sentence really says, "I do not care how this situation affects me, but I am concerned for others.")
Right: Within *himself,* a series of conflicts raged.

119. *Possessives—With Inanimate Objects*

The use of possessive forms with inanimate objects, i.e., objects without life, should be avoided if possible.

Undesirable: The *car's* hood is insulated.
Preferred: The *hood of the car* is insulated.
Undesirable: The *tree's* upper branches need pruning.
Preferred: The upper branches *of the tree* need pruning.

Note: There are many instances where the possessive with inanimate objects has become so firmly established that attempting to avoid the possessive would prove futile. Examples are: a day's work, a month's supply, a year's growth.

6

Errors in Using Verbs

The principal errors in the use of verbs can be classified logically under the following headings: (1) errors in agreement with subject; (2) errors in tense; (3) errors in voice; (4) errors in splitting forms; (5) errors in mood; and (6) miscellaneous errors.

Errors in agreement are treated under the section on "Errors in Using Nouns" (see pages 31-38). This section treats the other principal classifications.

TENSE

The term "tense" simply means time. Therefore, one establishes a time relationship in his speech or writing by using the proper tense of the verb.

In English, there are three primary tenses and three secondary tenses, with several variations on each of these six basic forms. The three primary tenses are the *present,* the *past,* and the *future.* The three secondary tenses are the *present perfect,* the *past perfect,* and the *future perfect.* Below are listed the forms of these six basic tenses.

The *present tense* is used to denote that which pertains to the present time.

I speak	we speak
you speak	you speak
he speaks	they speak

The *past tense* is used to denote that which pertains to the past time.

I spoke	we spoke
you spoke	you spoke
he spoke	they spoke

The *future tense* is used to denote that which pertains to a future time.

I shall speak	we shall speak
you will speak	you will speak
he will speak	they will speak

The *present perfect* tense is used to denote that which took place in the past but has consequences extending into the present. For example,

> I *have finished* my work. (The action of finishing is past. The consequences extending into the present are that I need not work any more because I have finished.)

The conjugation of the present perfect tense follows:

I have spoken	we have spoken
you have spoken	you have spoken
he has spoken	they have spoken

The *past perfect* tense is used to denote that which occurred before a specific moment in the past. For example,

> When you entered (the specific moment in the past), I *had finished* my work (the action before the specific moment in the past).

The conjugation of the past perfect follows:

I had spoken	we had spoken
you had spoken	you had spoken
he had spoken	they had spoken

The *future perfect* tense is used to denote that which will have occurred before a specific moment in the future.

> By the time you arrive tomorrow (the specific moment in the future), I *shall have finished* my work (the action that will have occurred before a specific moment in the future).

The conjugation of the future perfect follows:

I shall have finished	we shall have finished
you will have finished	you will have finished
he will have finished	they will have finished

In addition to knowing the uses of the six basic tenses, one must know the "principal parts" of verbs. The "principal parts" are simply the forms of the verb used with the various tenses. They are usually given under three headings—present, past, and past participle. However, these headings need some explanation.

The so-called "present form" is used with the present tense, but it is also used as part of the verb phrase in the future tense. For example,

> Today I *sing.* (Present tense)
>
> Tomorrow I *shall sing.* (Future tense)

The past form is used, as the name implies, to form the past tense (sometimes called the imperfect). For example,

> Yesterday I *sang.* (Past tense)

The past participle is used as part of the verb phrase for the three perfect tenses (present perfect, past perfect, future perfect).

> I have *sung.* (Present perfect)
>
> I had *sung.* (Past perfect)
>
> I shall have *sung.* (Future perfect)

Below are listed the three forms, i.e., the principal parts, of verbs most likely to present difficulty:

Present	Past	Past Participle
arise	arose	arisen
begin	began	begun
bid (command)	bade	bidden
bid (offer)	bid	bid
bite	bit	bit, bitten
blow	blew	blown
break	broke	broken
bring	brought	brought
burst	burst	burst
catch	caught	caught
choose	chose	chosen
come	came	come
dive	dived	dived

Present	Past	Past Participle
do	did	done
drag	dragged	dragged
draw	drew	drawn
drink	drank	drunk
drive	drove	driven
eat	ate	eaten
fall	fell	fallen
fly	flew	flown
forget	forgot	forgot, forgotten
freeze	froze	frozen
get	got	got
give	gave	given
go	went	gone
grow	grew	grown
hang (suspend)	hung	hung
hang (execute)	hanged	hanged
know	knew	known
lay (place)	laid	laid
lead	led	led
lend	lent	lent
lie (speak falsely)	lied	lied
lie (recline)	lay	lain
lose	lost	lost
pay	paid	paid
prove	proved	proved
raise	raised	raised
ride	rode	ridden
ring	rang, rung	rung
rise	rose	risen
run	ran	run
see	saw	seen
set	set	set
shake	shook	shaken
shrink	shrank	shrunk
sing	sang	sung
sink	sank	sunk

Present	*Past*	*Past Participle*
sit	sat	sat
speak	spoke	spoken
spring	sprang	sprung
steal	stole	stolen
swim	swam	swum
swing	swung	swung
take	took	taken
tear	tore	torn
throw	threw	thrown
wear	wore	worn
weave	wove	woven
wring	wrung	wrung
write	wrote	written

120. *Shift of Tense*

One must be careful to maintain consistency in his use of tense; he must not make an error in meaning by shifting tense.

Wrong: When I saw the lights coming toward the house, I *begin* to get afraid. (Wrong because "begin," which is a present tense, conflicts in meaning with "saw," which is a past tense.)

Right: When I saw the lights coming toward the house, I *began* to get afraid.

Wrong: I *should have liked to have heard* Caruso sing. (Wrong because the two present perfect constructions create a conflict that cannot be resolved.)

Right: I should like *to have heard* Caruso sing. (Right because action of "liking" is now present, thereby preventing a conflict with the present perfect "to have heard.")

Right: I *should have liked* to hear Caruso sing. (Right because the present perfect "have liked" does not conflict with the infinitive "to hear" which is not limited by tense.)

Wrong: When I come home at night, there she *will be* reading her newspaper.

Right: When I come home at night, there she *is* reading her newspaper.

Wrong: Last year when I *am* down in Texas, he *tells* the boss a lie.

Right: Last year when I *was* down in Texas, he *told* the boss a lie.

121. *General Truth*

The general truth, like the historical present (see below), requires the present tense.

The general truth is a fact that was true in the past, is true now, and in all probability will be true in the future. For example,

> Necessity *is* the mother of invention.

The general truth presents difficulty when it appears in a sentence with a past tense, because a tendency to use the past tense to express the general truth arises.

Wrong: Last week our clergyman reminded us that living the upright life *was* a discipline.

Right: Last week our clergyman reminded us that living the upright life *is* a discipline.

Wrong: Professor Jacques told us yesterday that iodine *was* effective in removing silver nitrate stains.

Right: Professor Jacques told us yesterday that iodine *is* effective in removing silver nitrate stains.

122. *Historical Present*

When speaking of a person or event which occupies a significant place in history, the present tense is employed. For example,

> Shakespeare *is* one of our greatest writers.

The use of the present tense to convey such a meaning is appropriately termed the "historical present."

Wrong: Abraham Lincoln *was* one of the great men in our history.

Right: Abraham Lincoln *is* one of the great men in our history.

Wrong: Ulysses S. Grant *ranked* as a poor president.

Right: Ulysses S. Grant *ranks* as a poor president.

Wrong: The Battle of Midway *was* a moment of which we can be proud.

Right: The Battle of Midway *is* a moment of which we can be proud.

123. *Confusing the Present Perfect with the Imperfect Tense (Past Tense)*

The present perfect tense, which is used to express action completed in the past with consequences extending into the present, is often confused with the imperfect which is used to express an indefinite past.

Wrong: Did you *finish* the work yet? (Wrong because a present perfect is needed to express the idea of consequences of a past action extending into the present.)
Right: Have you *finished* the work yet?
Wrong: Did Hal *bring* the car back yet?
Right: Has Hal *brought* the car back yet?
Wrong: Did Mrs. Meister, as of this moment, *complete* her work?
Right: Has Mrs. Meister, as of this moment, *completed* her work?

VOICE

124. *Shift from Active to Passive Voice*

The active voice is that in which the subject of the sentence performs the action. For example,

John *paints* the house.

The passive voice is that wherein the subject is acted upon. For example,

The house *was being painted.*

Although some authorities permit the shifting from active to passive voice within the sentence or the paragraph, most insist upon or recommend that such shifts be avoided.

Poor: The jockeys *were exercising* their horses; the troughs *were being filled* by the grooms; and the stable boys *were laying* out the harnesses. (Wrong because there is a shift from active to passive to active.)
Better: The jockeys *were exercising* their horses; the grooms *were filling* the troughs; and the stable boys *were laying* out the harnesses.

SPLIT FORMS

125. *Split Infinitives*

The infinitive is the "to" form of the verb, e.g., "to run," "to sing," "to drive," "to play." If a word is placed between the two words in the infinitive (e.g., "to *quickly* finish"), the infinitive is said to be "split."

Although some authorities approve of split infinitives, careful usage demands that splitting be avoided unless a strange or clumsy construction results.

Wrong: I plan *to hurriedly complete* the work and leave.
Right: I plan *to complete* the work hurriedly and leave.
Wrong: Mr. Jasper always likes *to closely examine* every report.
Right: Mr. Jasper always likes *to examine* closely every report.

Note: Sometimes an infinitive simply must be split to gain the meaning intended. Note the following:

Visitors are asked *to* please *park* their cars away from the main building.

In the sentence above, the word "please" must be placed within the infinitive so that it may modify the whole idea of being kind enough to park the cars away from the main building. Hence, in such an instance, the infinitive must be split.

126. *Split Verbs*

When a verb is composed of two or more words, the parts should not be split if such a splitting can be avoided.

Wrong: Mr. Kennedy *did,* I feel certain, *speak* on that subject before.
Right: Mr. Kennedy *did speak,* I feel certain, on that subject before.
Wrong: If I *am,* as you suggest, moving *illegally,* I shall cease.
Right: If, as you suggest, I *am moving* illegally, I shall cease.

Note: Occasionally the verb must be split. Some common examples are:

He *is* not *planning* any action.
Mary *was* never *cooking* at the right time.
Never *have* I really *seen* him.
Because I *was* barely *floundering,* I stopped to learn my mistake.

MOOD

The term "mood" refers exclusively to verbs. Mood is the property of the verb which reflects the manner in which the user conceives the verb. For example, if he wants to state an actual fact, he uses the indicative mood:

He *is* the instructor.
The horse *trots* slowly around the track.

If he wants to state (1) a wish or (2) a condition contrary to (opposed to) actual fact, he uses the *subjunctive* mood (see #127 shown below). If he wants to issue a command, he uses the imperative mood:

Stop that machine!
Give me the pen.

127. *Subjunctive Mood—Errors in Use of*

The subjunctive mood is used in English principally in two situations: (1) with the expression of a wish and (2) to express a condition contrary to actual fact. The present subjunctive is conjugated as follows:

I were	We were
You were	You were
He were	They were

The following is an example of the subjunctive mood used with the expression of a wish:

I wish he *were* there.

The following is an example of the subjunctive mood used to express a condition contrary to fact:

If he *were* here, he would help us.

Wrong: I wish I *was* as tall as my brother.
Right: I wish I *were* as tall as my brother.
Wrong: If Mary *was* here now, she would show you how to cook.
Right: If Mary *were* here now, she would show you how to cook.

128. *False Conditional*

When a speaker or writer wants to predicate a statement upon a hypothesis, he employs a subjunctive mood to establish the hypothesis (i.e., the situation contrary to fact), and he uses a conditional mood to express his statement (i.e., the statement predicated upon the assumption). For example, in the sentence,

If I *were* home, I *should be relaxing.*

the verb "were" is the subjunctive, and the verb phrase "should be relaxing" is the conditional.

If the conditional mood is to be used correctly, a condition contrary to fact must be involved. If no such condition is present, a very common error known as the "false conditional" results.

Wrong: When the boss entered the office in those days, Horton *would be working* very hard. (Wrong because "would be working" is a false conditional.)

Right: When the boss entered the office in those days, Horton *was* always *working* very hard.

Wrong: Every day when I arrived, he *would be* at his desk.

Right: Every day when I arrived, he *was* at his desk.

129. *Use of Indicative for Obligatory*

The common forms for expressing situations involving obligation or duty are "should," "ought," and "must." Examples are:

I *should mow* the lawn today.

He *ought* to help his neighbor.

We *must meet* our obligation.

A common error arises, however, in the practice of using an indicative to express obligation or duty.

Wrong: If he comes, *do* I tell him to remain?

Right: If he comes, *should* I tell him to remain?

Wrong: When the child disobeys, *does* the parent *chastise* him severely? (Wrong if obligation is involved. Right if no obligation is involved.)

Right: When the child disobeys, *should* the parent *chastise* him severely? (Right if obligation is involved.)

MISCELLANEOUS ERRORS

130. *Logical Arrangement of Verbs*

The arrangement of verbs in a sentence should be that of the actual sequence of events.

Wrong: He *ate, dressed,* and *washed* before seven o'clock. (Wrong unless this was the order of procedure.)
Right: He *washed, dressed,* and *ate* before seven o'clock.
Wrong: The car *slid, careened,* and *crashed* into the abutment. (Wrong unless it slid before it careened.)
Right: The car *careened, slid,* and *crashed* into the abutment.

131. *Don't–doesn't*

Confusion of the contractions "don't" and "doesn't" is quite common among those whose formal education has been limited.

The easiest course to follow in remembering which form to use is to substitute the full form ("do not," "does not") for the contracted form ("don't," "doesn't").

Wrong: He *don't* know the answer. (Wrong because "don't" really means "do not.")
Right: He *doesn't* know the answer.
Wrong: The baby *don't* look like his mother.
Right: The baby *doesn't* look like his mother.

132. *Curtailed Verbs*

In some localities, there is a tendency to curtail some verbs by dropping a letter or a syllable.

Wrong: We were *suppose* to help each other.
Right: We were *supposed* to help each other.
Wrong: He never *expect* us to stay.
Right: He never *expected* us to stay.

Note: Some localities also use certain verbs in individual patterns, thereby creating localisms. In formal usage, therefore, one must beware such constructions as:

I don't guess Conway will be there.

We'll doze (bulldoze) the debris.

Jerry will gas up the car for the trip.

7

Errors Arising from the Confusion of Adjectives and Adverbs

In order to avoid mistakes in the use of the adjective and the adverb, one must (1) know the definition of the adjective and of the adverb, (2) be able to recognize which form is needed in every instance, and (3) know the proper adjectival and adverbial forms of the particular word.

An adjective is a word that modifies (i.e., tells something about or limits in some way) a noun or a pronoun. In the following sentence, "tired" and "beaten" modify the noun "team":

The *tired, beaten* team trotted slowly off the field.

An adverb is a word that modifies a verb, an adjective, or another adverb.

He works *rapidly.* ("rapidly" modifies the verb "works.")
He is a *fairly* rapid worker. ("fairly" modifies the adjective "rapid.")
He works *fairly* rapidly. ("fairly" modifies the adverb "rapidly.")

This section treats errors arising from the confusion of adjectival and adverbial forms. Errors in the use of the predicate adjective are treated separately in the section following this. (See page 71.)

133. *Easy—easily*

"Easy" is an adjective; "easily" is an adverb.

Wrong: He decided to work *slow* and *easy.* (Wrong because the adverbial form is needed to modify the verb phrase "decided to work.")
Right: He decided to work *slowly* and *easily.*

134. *Good—well*

"Good" is an adjective; "well" is an adverb.

Wrong: He played *good* in every game. (Wrong because the adverbial form is needed to modify the verb "played.")
Right: He played *well* in every game.
Right: He was a *good* player in every game. ("good" is used correctly as an adjective modifying the noun "player.")

135. *Quick—quickly*

"Quick" is an adjective; "quickly" is an adverb.

Wrong: He worked *quick* in order to avoid detection. (Wrong because the adverbial form is needed to modify the verb "worked.")
Right: He worked *quickly* in order to avoid detection.

136. *Slow—slowly*

"Slow" is an adjective; "slowly" is an adverb.

Wrong: He walked *slow* in order to arrive after ten o'clock. (Wrong because the adverbial form is needed to modify the verb "walked.")
Right: He walked *slowly* in order to arrive after ten o'clock.
Wrong: If we can work *slow* and *steady,* we can finish by noon.
Right: If we can work *slowly* and *steadily,* we can finish by noon.
Wrong: Striking *slow* and *even,* the village clock sounded midnight.
Right: Striking *slowly* and *evenly,* the village clock sounded midnight.

Note: Notwithstanding the many traffic signs throughout the Nation, the following sentence is wrong:

Drive *slow!*

137. *Real—really*

"Real" is an adjective; "really" is an adverb.

Wrong: We had a *real* good time. (Wrong because an adverbial form is needed to modify the adjective "good.")
Right: We had a *really* good time.
Wrong: The team played *real* good for the first five minutes.
Right: The team played *really* well for the first five minutes.

138. *Some—somewhat*

Some is an adjective of indefinite number. It is used correctly in the following instances:

> I have *some* paper left.
>
> *Some* friends of his were there.

"Some" should not be confused with the adverb "somewhat."

Wrong: He is *some* better today. (An adverb is needed to modify the adjective "better.")

Right: He is *somewhat* better today.

Wrong: He harangued *some* after you left.

Right: He harangued for a *short while* after you left.

Dialect: That was *some* car you were driving!

Better: That was a *striking* car you were driving!

8

Errors in Using the Predicate Adjective

In order to understand the common errors in the use of the predicate adjective, one must first understand the nature of the predicate adjective itself.

A predicate adjective is an adjective in the part of the sentence from the verb onward when the sentence is arranged in its natural order (the predicate) which modifies a noun or pronoun acting as the subject of the verb. For example:

> The man looked *sad*. ("sad" is a predicate adjective modifying the noun "man" which is the subject of the verb "looked.")
>
> The captain was *tired*. ("tired" modifies "captain.")
>
> The juice tasted *sweet*. ("sweet" modifies "juice.")

The following illustrate common errors in the use of the predicate adjective.

139. *Feel bad* versus *feel badly*

"Bad" is an adjective; "badly" is an adverb.

Wrong: I feel *badly*. ("badly" is wrong because in this instance a predicate adjective is needed to modify the pronoun "I." Hence, "bad" must be substituted for "badly.")

Right: I feel *bad*. ("bad" is correct because, as shown above, it modifies the subject pronoun "I.")

Wrong: He feels *badly* about his son's injury.

Right: He feels *bad* about his son's injury.

Note: In the rare instance where the verb "feel" is to be modified, an adverb naturally must be used. For example, a blind man speaking

71

of his inability to feel the raised letters in a book printed in Braille might say,

I feel *badly* today.

140. *Due to—because of*

Whenever the expression "due to" is used, the word "due" must be a predicate adjective. The expression "due to" must not be used synonymously with the expression "because of," which is a prepositional construction, i.e., does the work of a preposition.

Wrong: We were late *due to* the blowout. (Wrong because "due" is not a predicate adjective as it must be when it is used in the phrase "due to.")

Right: We were late *because of* the blowout. (Right because the prepositional construction "because of" is needed rather than the construction "due to" which can never do the work of a preposition.

Right: Our lateness was *due to* the blowout. (Right because in this sentence "due" is a predicate adjective modifying the noun "lateness.")

Wrong: The highways were slippery *due to* the ice.

Right: The highways were slippery *because of* the ice.

Note: A fact worth remembering is that a sentence must never begin with the expression "due to."

Wrong: *Due to* the weather, there was a large crowd.

Right: *Because of* the weather, there was a large crowd.

141. *Prior to—before*

The expression "prior to" is similar to the expression "due to"; that is, when the expression "prior to" is used correctly, "prior" must be a predicate adjective. Also, the expression "prior to" cannot be used as a prepositional construction to be substituted for the preposition "before."

Wrong: Our first meeting was scheduled *prior to* May 15, 1961. (Wrong because "prior to" is being used synonymously with "before," which is a preposition.)

Right: Our first meeting was scheduled *before* May 15, 1961.

Wrong: The letter came *prior to* the package.

Right: The letter came *before* the package.

Right: The arrival of the letter was *prior to* that of the package. (Right because "prior" is a predicate adjective.)

Note: As is true of "due to," "prior to" can never begin a sentence.

Wrong: Prior to the winter, we repaired the roof.

Right: Before the winter, we repaired the roof.

142. *Sensory Verbs with the Predicate Adjective*

A sensory verb is one which pertains to the senses—seeing, hearing, feeling, tasting, smelling, etc.

When a modifier is used after a sensory verb, one must be certain that he has made the right choice. For example,

> He looked *sad.*

is correct because "sad" is a predicate adjective modifying the subject pronoun "he." However,

> He looked *sadly* about the room.

is also correct because "sadly" is an adverb modifying the verb "looked."

Sensory verbs often present difficulty in choosing between an adjective and an adverb. Nevertheless, if one remembers the many instances in which he normally uses predicate adjectives correctly after sensory verbs, he will have a sound basis for using the predicate adjective correctly. The following are instances of daily use of the predicate adjective after sensory verbs. All, of course, are correct.

> The juice tastes *sour.*
> The flower smells *sweet.*
> I feel *tired.*
> Joe looks *strong* again.
> The newcomer appears *strange.*

The following sentences illustrate common errors in the use of the predicate adjective.

Wrong: He looked *differently* after his return from Europe. (Wrong because a predicate adjective is needed to modify the subject pronoun "he.")

Right: He looked *different* after his return from Europe.
Wrong: He feels *badly* about the defeat. (Predicate adjective needed.)
Right: He feels *bad* about the defeat.
Wrong: The cider tasted *badly*. (Predicate adjective needed.)
Right: The cider tasted *bad*.

Note: A knowledge of "linking" verbs proves helpful in handling predicate adjectives.

A linking verb is one which does not refer to something which the subject does or experiences; rather, it merely links the subject to other words. The common linking verbs are the common forms of the verb "to be" (am, is, are, was, were, be, been); the verb "seem"; and several verbs which can function as linking verbs ("became," "turned," "grew," "proved," etc.).

The linking verb must be recognized because it frequently is followed by a predicate adjective.

Right: He became *strong* and *reliable*. ("Strong" and "reliable" are predicate adjectives modifying the pronoun "he.")
Right: The witness turned *pale* as the prosecutor continued his cross-examination.
Right: Marston proved *steady* and *consistent* in the long run.
Right: Little **Humphrey** grew *thoughtful* and *courteous* as the years passed.

9

Errors in Using Adverbs

143. *Adverb—Mistaking for a Pronoun*

Many persons use an adverbial modifier when a substantive (noun, pronoun, or group of words acting as a noun) is needed.

Wrong: My greatest thirst is *when* I work hard in a strong sun. (Wrong because the user is attempting to equate "thirst," a noun, with "when I work hard in a strong sun," which is an adverbial phrase.)
Right: My greatest thirst is *that which* comes when I work hard in a strong sun.
Right: My greatest thirst comes *when* I work hard in a strong sun.
Wrong: Mr. Powell's realization of defeat *was after* the judge announced his ruling.
Right: Mr. Powell's realization of defeat *came after* the judge announced his ruling.
Right: Mr. Powell realized his defeat *after* the judge announced his ruling.

144. *Is when—is where*

"When" and "where" are generally adverbs. Consequently they cannot be used to introduce noun clauses.

Wrong: Erosion *is where* the soil is washed away.
Right: Erosion occurs *when* the soil is washed away.
Right: Erosion has occurred *where* the soil is washed away.
Wrong: A fatality *is where* someone has been killed.
Right: A fatality *is* an instance in which someone is killed.
Wrong: Illiteracy is *when* a man cannot read or write.
Right: Illiteracy is the *condition* of the man who cannot read or write.

Wrong: Now is *when* he should be on hand.
Right: Now is the *time* when he should be on hand.

145. *Reason why—reason that*

The word "why" is an adverb; the word "that" is either a pronoun or an adjective, according to its use.

A common error arises in the use of the adverb "why" for the relative pronoun "that."

Wrong: The reason *why* he came is that he needs rest.
Right: The reason *that* he came is that he needs rest.
Wrong: This is the reason *why* I am working.
Right: This is the reason *that* I am working.

Note: The above discussion treats the incorrect use of "why" as a pronoun. However, there is a closely related situation in which "why" is part adverb and part conjunction. This situation is frequently termed the "conjunctive adverb." Note that in the following sentences the "why" is actually part adverb and part conjunction.

Right: I never knew *why* he came.
Right: The president explained *why* he was not interested in the plan.
Right: *Why* he is here I am unable to say.

146. *What for—why*

The expression "what for" must not be used as a substitute for the adverb "why."

Wrong: What did you paint the house white *for?*
Right: *Why* did you paint the house white?
Wrong: *What* did he go to Europe during the winter *for?*
Right: *Why* did he go to Europe during the winter?

147. *Where—for that*

The adverb "where" must not be used for the relative pronoun "that."

Wrong: I see in this book *where* the city of Dallas has a large museum.
Right: I see in this book *that* the city of Dallas has a large museum.

Note: The error below is also commonly made.

Wrong: Here is *where* he lives.
Right: He lives *here.*

148. *Where—Use of Interrogatively*

When the adverb "where" is used interrogatively, it should not be accompanied by the preposition "at."

Wrong: Where is the house *at?*
Right: Where is the house?
Wrong: Where did you see the deer *at* when you were hunting?
Right: Where did you see the deer when you were hunting?

10

Errors in Using Modifying Elements

The term "modifying element" refers to words and groups of words which describe or limit.

Modifying elements are essential to the meaning of sentences. This section discusses the common errors made in handling them.

149. Modifiers—Position of According to Length

Whenever possible, modifiers should be arranged according to length, with the shortest preceding the others.

Uneven: It was a *battered, worn, broken* desk.
Better: It was a *worn, broken, battered* desk.
Uneven: He was *disheveled, dirty,* and *untidy.*
Better: He was *dirty, untidy,* and *disheveled.*
Uneven: He spoke *meditatively, frankly,* and *sincerely.*
Better: He spoke *frankly, sincerely,* and *meditatively.*

150. Modifiers—Sequence of

Modifiers should always be arranged in logical sequence.

Wrong: As the days wore on, he became *tired, bored,* and *exhausted.*
 (Wrong because he probably became bored before he became tired.)
Right: As the days wore on, he became *bored, tired,* and *exhausted.*
Wrong: The grass became *withered, dry,* and *flaky.*
Right: The grass became *dry, withered,* and *flaky.*
Wrong: The students became *angered, annoyed,* and *enraged.*
Right: The students became *annoyed, angered,* and *enraged.*

151. *Modifiers—Double Negative*

Some modifiers have a distinctly negative meaning, and consequently they should not be used as modifiers of another negative word. When this situation occurs, a double negative is created. (See page 131 for an explanation of "double negative.")

Wrong: We *haven't scarcely* any sugar. (Wrong because "scarcely" conveys a negative meaning thereby creating a double negative.)
Right: We have *scarcely* any sugar.
Wrong: They *can't hardly* speak English.
Right: They can *hardly* speak English.
Wrong: He *didn't* speak *but* once.
Right: He spoke *but* once.
Wrong: The guard *didn't barely* touch the player.
Right: The guard *barely* touched the player.

152. *Modifiers—Incorrectly Written*

Even the most careful of speakers and writers occasionally find that they have cast a modifying element incorrectly. They express a thought correctly, they believe, only to realize later that their sentence has not conveyed the meaning they intended.

The following sentences contain incorrectly used modifying elements.

Wrong: When he was four years old, the boy's father died. (According to this sentence, the boy's father died at age four.)
Right: When the boy was four years old, his father died.
Wrong: Before he was born, Lem's uncle decided to change his will in favor of Lem. (According to this sentence, Lem's uncle made his decision before being born.)
Right: Before Lem was born, his uncle decided to change his will in Lem's favor.

153. *Modifiers—Misplaced Clause*

The misplaced modifying clause may be corrected by simply changing its position or recasting the sentence.

Wrong: There was a maverick beside the bush *which the cowboy lassoed.* (Wrong because as this sentence stands the cowboy lassoed the bush. If, of course, the user wants this unusual meaning, the sentence is correct.)

Right: The cowboy lassoed a maverick which was beside the bush.
Wrong: It was the third fish on the platter *that he ate.*
Right: He ate the third fish on the platter.

154. *Modifiers—Misplaced Word*

In using single words as modifiers, one must be careful to see that they modify the proper word. Otherwise, the sentence, while grammatically acceptable, will create a meaning other than that intended by the speaker or writer. Notice that each of the following sentences is grammatically acceptable; but notice also the different meaning created by the difference in position of the word "nearly."

> The farmer *nearly* lost one hundred cattle in the fire.
> The farmer lost *nearly* one hundred cattle in the fire.

According to the first sentence, the farmer lost no cattle. According to the second, he lost a number in excess of ninety.

Wrong: I *only* whispered to Ollie. (Wrong unless the user means "I did not speak in a conversational tone, a shout, or anything other than a whisper.")
Right: I whispered *only* to Ollie. (Right if the user means that Ollie was the only person to whom he whispered.)
Wrong: He *only* ate salad and a roll for lunch.
Right: He ate *only* a salad and a roll for lunch.
Wrong: Last year I *almost* earned $15,000.
Right: Last year I earned *almost* $15,000.

155. *Modifiers—Misplaced Phrase*

Like the misplaced modifying clause, the misplaced modifying phrase can be corrected by changing its position or by recasting the sentence.

Wrong: He told me what to do *with a smile.*
Right: He told me *with a smile* what to do.
Wrong: The man spoke to the lion *with a cigar in the corner of* his mouth.
Right: The man *with a cigar in the corner of his mouth* spoke to the lion.

156. *Modifiers—Dangling*

The term "dangling modifier" refers to the modifier which does not function properly because one or more words have been omitted.

Wrong: While dressing, the alarm clock went off. (Wrong because the phrase "while dressing" modifies "clock.")
Right: While I was dressing, the alarm clock went off.
Wrong: Walking down the road, a grocery was seen.
Right: Walking down the road, I saw a grocery.
Right: As I walked down the road, I saw a grocery.

157. *Modifiers—Squinting*

A squinting modifier is one which can modify either of the two elements between which it is placed. Notice how the adverb "slowly" in the following sentence can modify either the idea of "cooking" or the idea of "became noticeable."

The aroma of the food that he was cooking *slowly* became noticeable.

The term "squinting" is used to cover this situation because the adverb attempts to look or "squint" in two directions.

Wrong: Mr. Jones' habit of speaking *rapidly* impressed the visitor.
Right: Mr. Jones' *habit of rapid speech* impressed the visitor.
Right: Mr. Jones' habit of speech *rapidly impressed* the visitor.
Wrong: Driving to town *for them* became a necessity.
Right: *For them,* driving to town became a necessity.
Right: The necessity arose of driving to town *for them.*

II

Errors in Using Prepositions

158. *Prepositions—Ending Sentences with*

In days gone by, teachers of grammar strenuously objected to the practice of ending sentences with prepositions. Now, however, the practice is completely acceptable as a means of avoiding awkward sentence structure, but only for this reason.

The following sentences illustrate acceptable instances of ending sentences with prepositions:

The watchman seemed to know what the sign stood *for.*

The customer invariably gets what he pays *for.*

The following sentences illustrate instances where the ending of a sentence with a preposition can be avoided.

Acceptable: This is the table I am planning to put the vase *on.*
Better: This is the table *on which* I am planning to put the vase.
Acceptable: I really don't know what I am here *for.*
Better: I really don't know *why* I am here.
Acceptable: We received everything we asked *for.*
Better: We received everything we *requested.*
Acceptable: Whom should I give the parcel *to?*
Better: To whom should I give the parcel?

159. *Suspended Prepositional Phrases*

A suspended prepositional phrase occurs when a given noun or pronoun serves as the object of two prepositions. Therefore the meaning of the first prepositional phrase is not clear until the end of the second phrase is reached. For example:

We are interested *in* and indebted *to* the boy.

In this sentence, "boy" is the object of the preposition "in" and the preposition "to." The words "and indebted to," therefore, suspend the preposition "in" from its object "boy."

Some authorities condemn the suspended prepositional phrase under any circumstances. If, however, one insists on using the suspended prepositional phrase, he must guard against omitting either of the prepositions.

Wrong: He had a need and interest *in* athletics. (Wrong because no preposition is stated after "need." Therefore, it is assumed to be "in.")

Right: He had a need *for* and an interest *in* athletics.

Wrong: We must guard and cast aside *any* infringement on our rights.

Right: We must guard *against* and cast *aside* any infringement on our rights.

160. *Double Prepositions*

The double preposition is sometimes correct and sometimes incorrect. The following are instances of correct use of double prepositions.

> He stepped *out of* the car.
> He walked *up to* the stage.
> He came *over to* the house.

It should be noted that some grammarians consider the first of these prepositions as adverbs, while other grammarians consider the two words as a single preposition. This second group terms the two words "phrasal prepositions" or "double prepositions." Whatever one's view may be, he must avoid the errors shown below.

Wrong: Mother was looking *out of* the window.
Right: Mother was looking *out* the window.
Wrong: Little Roberta fell *off of* the top step.
Right: Little Roberta fell *off* the top step.
Wrong: The fisherman put the boat *up under* the dock.
Right: The fisherman put the boat *under* the dock.
Wrong: I shall be there at *about* ten o'clock.
Right: I shall be there *about* ten o'clock.
Right: I shall be there *at* ten o'clock.

161. *Blame on—blame it on*

Formal usage requires the use of the preposition "for" with the verb "blame" in instances where a preposition is needed.

Wrong: He blamed the accident *on* Bestor.
Right: He blamed Bestor *for* the accident.
Wrong: Please don't blame it *on* Morton.
Right: Please don't *blame* Morton.

162. *Differ from—differ with*

"Differ from" means to be "dissimilar." For example,

This book differs *from* that one.

"Differ with" means to "disagree with someone." For example,

I differ *with* Mr. Jackson on that question.

Wrong: Mr. Jay differs *from* Mr. Thomson on that point. (Wrong if disagreement is meant. Right if dissimilarity is meant.)
Right: Mr. Jay differs *with* Mr. Thomson on that point.

163. *Different from—different than*

A common error arises with the "different from" construction. This error can be avoided if one remembers that the word "from" is a preposition, and the word "than" is a conjunction. Hence in the following sentence,

This car is different *from* that car.

the preposition "from" is needed to establish the relationship between the word "car" (the second "car") and the word "different." If the conjunction "than" were used in place of "from," the sentence would read

This car is different than that car is different.

Obviously this second sentence does not make sense. Therefore, the first sentence is correct.

Wrong: This highway is different *than* that highway.
Right: This highway is different *from* that highway.
Wrong: My house is different *than* your house in several ways.

Right: My house is different *from* your house in several ways.
Right: My house *differs from* your house in several ways.

164. *Of—Unnecessary Use of*

The preposition "of" is often incorrectly used with verbs. Listed below are some common instances of this error.

Wrong: Keep *off of* the grass.
Right: Keep *off* the grass.
Wrong: Father was gazing *out of* the transom.
Right: Father was gazing *out* the transom.
Wrong: The car was *alongside of* the garage.
Right: The car was *alongside* the garage.

165. *Of—Used as a Substitute for "Have"*

The use of the preposition "of" for the auxiliary "have" is an inexcusable error.

Wrong: I could *of* had three more helpers.
Right: I could *have* had three more helpers.
Wrong: He must *of* known the answer.
Right: He must *have* known the answer.

166. *Up—Unnecessary Use of*

Although the preposition "up" is sometimes used idiomatically with verbs (e.g., "break *up*," "live *up* to reputation," "stand *up* to accusers"), it is often used unnecessarily with verbs. The following represent common errors.

Wrong: We shall divide *up* the pie among us boys.
Right: We shall *divide* the pie among us boys.
Wrong: We shall stack *up* the dishes.
Right: We shall *stack* the dishes.
Wrong: The thirsty children drank *up* all the lemonade.
Right: The thirsty children *drank* all the lemonade.
Wrong: He couldn't think *up* an answer.
Right: He couldn't *find* (invent) an answer.
Wrong: Mrs. Casey is planning to do *up* her house.
Right: Mrs. Casey is planning to *decorate* her house.

167. *Up—Separating from Verb*

If the preposition "up" is to be used with a verb, it should not be needlessly separated from the verb.

Wrong: The highwayman *held* the roofer *up*.
Right: The highwayman *held up* the roofer.
Wrong: The mechanic *tuned* the motor *up*.
Right: The mechanic *tuned up* the motor.

168. *With* and *To—Use of*

Authorities have dictated the use of certain prepositions in specific instances. Although these uses may not seem logical, one must nonetheless learn them as he learns other idioms. Among the most troublesome are the rules treated in this section.

One becomes angry *with* persons but *at* situations.

Wrong: I was angry *at* my brother.
Right: I was angry *with* my brother.
Wrong: I was angry *with* the results.
Right: I was angry *at* the results.

One may compare an object "to" or "with" another.

Right: I am comparing this collar *with* that collar.
Right: I am comparing this collar *to* that collar.

In the strictest sense, the word "to" when used with numbers does not include the second number stated.

Wrong: If one is asked to count from one to five, he should count as
follows; one, two, three, four, *five*.
Right: If one is asked to count from one to five, he should count as
follows; one, two, three, four.
Right: If one is asked to count from one to five *inclusive,* he should
count as follows; one, two, three, four, five.

When used with verbs of speaking (talk, speak, etc.), the preposition "to" indicates that one person did all the speaking. For example,

I spoke *to* the group. ("I" did all the talking.)

The preposition "with," on the other hand, conveys the idea of at least a two-way discussion. For example,

I spoke *with* the group about their problem.

This sentence conveys the idea of a discussion between the speaker and the group.

Wrong: I spoke *to* my son about his course selections for next year.
　　(Wrong if the parent gave the son an opportunity to speak.)
Right: I spoke *with* my son about his course selections for next year.

ADDENDUM

Below are two miscellaneous problems that often arise with the use of the preposition.

Occasionally a redundancy occurs with the use of two prepositions in the same phrase. Note the redundancy in these widely used phrases: "over and above political trends;" "behind and beyond the immediate facts;" "carried by and with the storm;" "known by and for his powerful voice."

The words "on" and "to" sometimes present the question of writing them as one word or two. Examine this sentence:

We drove on to the town.

Notice how "on" is an adverb because it tells where we drove (i.e., modifies "drove") while "to" is a preposition because it shows the relationship between the verb "drove" and the noun "town."

Here, then, is a rule: when "on" is an adverb and "to" is a preposition, write them as separate words.

Now examine this sentence:

We drove onto the bridge.

Notice how "onto" is a preposition—and hence written as a single word—because it shows the relationship between "drove" and "bridge."

12

Errors in Using Conjunctions

169. *As . . . as—so . . . as*

One of the marks of the careful speaker and writer is the proper use of the correlative conjunctions "as . . . as" and "so . . . as." Although some authorities no longer insist on a distinction in the use of these forms, precise usage demands that "as . . . as" be used in positive situations and "so . . . as" in negative situations.

Wrong: He is *not as* tall as his father. (Wrong because this is a negative situation.)
Right: He is *not so* tall as his father.
Wrong: Carl is not *as* reliable *as* Leo.
Right: Carl is *not so* reliable as Leo.
Right: Houser is *as* strong *as* Dawkins.
Right: Perkins is *as* capable *as* Conners.

170. *As—Omission of*

When employing the correlative conjunctions "as . . . as," one must be careful not to omit the second "as."

Wrong: This rake is *as* good if not better than the old one.
Right: This rake is *as* good *as* if not better than the old one.

Note: Many authorities insist on considering the phrase "if not better than" as a parenthetical element. Therefore, they punctuate the sentence above in this way:

This rake is as good as, if not better than, the old one.

The punctuation of this construction is treated on page 105.

Wrong: Young is *as* reliable and in some ways more reliable than Moe.
Right: Young is *as* reliable *as* and in some ways more reliable than Moe.

171. *As—Used as a Synonym for "That" or "Whether"*

"As" may not be used as a substitute for the words "that" or "whether."

Wrong: I don't know *as* I shall go.
Right: I don't know *whether* (or *that*) I shall go.
Wrong: I am not sure *as* he is the man we need.
Right: I am not sure *whether* (or *that*) he is the man we need.

172. *Either . . . or—neither . . . nor*

When one uses the correlative conjunctions "either . . . or" and "neither . . . nor," he must be certain to use "or" with "either" and "nor" with "neither."

Wrong: Neither John *or* I am to receive the award.
Right: Neither John *nor* I am to receive the award.
Wrong: Either Josephs *nor* I am not going.
Right: Neither Josephs *nor* I am going.

Note: The verb following the second noun or pronoun always agrees in person and number with the noun preceding it, as was explained on page 40. Therefore,

Neither Sarah nor I *am* capable.
Neither Sarah nor he *is* capable.
Neither they nor we *are* capable.

173. *Either* and *Neither—Number Involved in*

The words "either" and "neither" should be used when only *two* persons or ideas are involved. If three or more persons or ideas are involved, the use of the words "either" or "neither" is incorrect.

Wrong: Either Harold, Dick, or Russ will help with the work. (Wrong because three persons are involved.)
Right: Harold, Dick, or Russ will help with the work.
Right: Either Harold or Dick will help with the work. (Right because only two persons are involved.)

Wrong: Neither the truck, the station wagon, nor the sports car will be there.

Right: The truck, the station wagon, and/or the sports car will not be there.

Right: Neither the truck nor the station wagon will be there.

174. *Either . . . or* and *Neither . . . nor—Relationship of Pronouns to*

When a pronoun has as its antecedent a noun or pronoun located in an "either . . . or" or a "neither . . . nor" construction, the second named noun or pronoun is considered the antecedent. The second named noun or pronoun, therefore, governs the person and the number of the following pronoun.

Wrong: Either Joe or Walter must raise *their* hand as a signal. (Wrong because the second named noun, "Walter," is third person singular.)

Right: Either Joe or Walter must raise *his* hand as a signal.

Wrong: Neither Hal nor Oscar was in *their* place.

Right: Neither Hal nor Oscar was in *his* place.

Right: Either Patterson or the Smith twins must accept *their* responsibilities.

Right: Either the Smith twins or Patterson must accept *his* responsibility.

175. *Except*

The word "except" is generally either a preposition or a verb. It is never a conjunction.

Wrong: He will not do the work *except* I give the order. (Wrong because "except" is being used as a conjunction.)

Right: He will not do the work *unless* I give the order.

Wrong: Henry does not eat *except* it is meal time.

Right: Henry does not eat *unless* it is meal time.

176. *If*

The subordinate conjunction "if" conveys the idea of a condition. It should not be confused with the subordinate conjunction "whether" or the relative pronoun "that."

Wrong: I don't know *if* snow is falling. (Wrong because no condition is involved.)
Right: I don't know *whether* snow is falling.
Wrong: We are not sure *if* he is coming.
Right: We are not sure *that* he is coming.
Wrong: Mother wants to know *if* Joe has arrived.
Right: Mother wants to know *whether* Joe has arrived.

177. *Like*

The word "like" is either a verb or a preposition. It is never a conjunction.

Wrong: He runs *like* I do. (Wrong because "like" is being used as a conjunction.)
Right: He runs *as* I do.
Right: He runs *like* me. (Actually, this form is idiomatic. It is correct because "like" is used as a preposition.)
Wrong: It looks *like* it's going to rain.
Right: It looks *like* rain.
Wrong: Mary looks *like* she is a lady in distress.
Right: Mary looks *like* a lady in distress.

178. *Without*

"Without" is a preposition. Therefore, it must not be used as a conjunction.

Wrong: He will not bring the car here *without* I tell him. (Wrong because "without" is being used as a conjunction.)
Right: He will not bring the car here *without my telling* him. (Right because "without" is used correctly as a preposition. Its object is the gerund "telling.")
Wrong: Oswald will not follow the order *without* the captain tells him.
Right: Oswald will not follow the order *unless* the captain tells him.

179. *Than—Pronoun Following*

The word "than" is a conjunction. Therefore, one must be careful to supply the words that are understood (if any) after it. For example, in the sentence,

He is taller than I.

the words "am tall" are understood after the pronoun. Therefore, the pronoun must be "I" rather than "me."

Wrong: The Clegg brothers are more reliable than *them.* (Wrong because "them" cannot serve as the subject of the verb "are" which is understood.)

Right: The Clegg brothers are more reliable than *they.*

Wrong: I have more mistakes on my paper than *him.*

Right: I have more mistakes on my paper than *he.*

Note: The use of "different than" instead of "different from" is discussed on page 84.

13

Errors in Making Comparisons

In making comparisons, one must know the basic facts of the so-called "three degrees of comparison."

The first is the *positive* degree. It is used in speaking of *one* person, idea, or object only. For example,

> He is a *slow* worker.
> This is an *expensive* book.

The second is the *comparative* degree. It is used when one is speaking of *two* persons, ideas, or objects.

> He is a *slower* worker than Lester.
> This is a *more expensive* book than that one.

The third is the superlative degree. It is used when one is speaking of *three or more* persons, ideas, or objects.

> He is the *slowest* of the workers.
> This is the *most expensive* of the books under consideration.

Below are illustrated the most common errors in using the three degrees of comparison.

180. *Confusion of Degrees of Comparison*

Wrong: He is the *poorest* of the two goalies on the squad. (Wrong because a comparative, rather than a superlative, form is needed.)

Right: He is the *poorer* of the goalies on the squad. (Note that the word "two" has been dropped because the comparative form "poorer" implies two. Thus "two" becomes redundant.)

Wrong: She is the *prettiest* twin.

Right: She is the *prettier* twin.
Wrong: This is the *least* expensive of the two cars.
Right: This is the *less* expensive of the cars.

181. *Language Errors in Making Comparisons*

When making comparisons, one must be certain that his language conveys his precise meaning.

Wrong: The *habits* of Copperheads are different from *Diamond Backs.* (Wrong because as this sentence stands "habits" are being compared with "Diamond Backs.")
Right: The *habits* of Copperheads are different from *those* of Diamond Backs.
Wrong: Chicago is larger than *any city* in Illinois. (Wrong. Since Chicago itself is in Illinois, the sentence actually says that "Chicago is larger than Chicago.")
Right: Chicago is larger than *any other* city in Illinois.
Wrong: John is taller than *any boy* in the class. (Wrong if John *is* a member of the class. However, this sentence is right if John is *not* a member of the class.)
Right: John is taller than *any other* boy in the class.
Right: London is larger than *any* city in Brazil. (Right because London is not in Brazil.)

182. *Errors in Comparing Adjectives*

An "absolute" is an adjective or an adverb which cannot be compared because it is complete. For example, the adjective "circular" is absolute because an object is either circular or it is not; it cannot be "more" or "most" circular.

To convey the idea that one object is closer to an absolute condition than is a second object, the expression "more nearly" is employed. For example,

This desk is *more nearly* circular than that one.

To convey the idea that one object is more removed from an absolute condition than is a second object, the expression "less nearly" is employed. For example,

That desk is *less nearly* circular than this one.

Common errors in the use of absolute adjectives are illustrated in the following sentences.

Wrong: This box is *more square* than that one.
Right: This box is *more nearly* square than that one.
Wrong: This box is *less square* than that one.
Right: This box is *less nearly* square than that one.
Wrong: These lines are *more parallel* than those.
Right: These lines are *more nearly parallel* than those.
Wrong: These lines are *less parallel* than those.
Right: These lines are *less nearly parallel* than those.
Wrong: This dog is *deader* than that dog.
Right: This dog *has been dead* longer than that dog.
Wrong: Our work is the *most vital* in the entire program.
Right: Our work is the *most important* (*most significant* or similar term) in the entire program.
Wrong: This task is the *most essential* function in the operation.
Right: This task is *essential* in the operation.

183. *Double Comparative*

The double comparative consists of using two comparatives to make a single comparison.

Wrong: The metal covering was *more stronger* than the wooden covering.
Right: The metal covering was *stronger* than the wooden covering.
Wrong: The old car moved *much more faster* than the new car.
Right: The old car moved *much faster* than the new car.

184. *False Comparisons*

A false comparison is one wherein a comparative or a superlative degree construction is used without a clearly stated basis for the comparison; that is to say, the person, object, or idea to which the second is being compared is not clear.

Although colloquial English sanctions the use of an incomplete or false comparison, formal English does not. Below are examples of false comparison, followed by the correct form.

Wrong: She is a *most beautiful* woman.
Right: She is a *very beautiful* woman.

Wrong: This is a *most satisfactory* car.
Right: This is a *highly satisfactory* car.
Wrong: Parker is one of our *better* students.
Right: Parker is one of our *superior* students.

185. *Incomplete Comparison Resulting from Ellipsis*

The speaker and the writer must be careful not to omit words which make a comparison incomplete or give a meaning other than the one intended.

Wrong: I like her *more than* Sally. (Wrong because the omission of words leaves the listener or the reader in doubt about the intended meaning.)
Right: I like her *more than I like* Sally. (If this is the meaning intended.)
Right: I like her *more than Sally likes* her. (If this is the meaning intended.)
Wrong: We gave Carter *more* votes *than* Perkins.
Right: We gave Carter *more* votes *than we gave* Perkins.
Right: We gave Carter *more* votes *than Perkins gave* Carter.

Note: The following incomplete comparisons are widely used in conversation, but they should not be used in writing.

Wrong: As a lecturer, Professor Smith is *so bad.*
Right: As a lecturer, Professor Smith is *so bad that* he bores us.
Wrong: She is *such* a pleasant girl to know.
Right: She is *such* a pleasant girl *that* we enjoy knowing her.
Wrong: Albert is not *too* intelligent.
Right: Albert is *not superior* in intelligence.

186. *All the Farther, All the Faster, etc.*

The expression "all the" combined with a comparative dagree modifier has a fairly wide acceptance. However, this expression should be avoided in formal discourse.

Wrong: Page ten was *all the farther* he studied.
Right: He did not study *beyond* page ten.
Wrong: Forty miles an hour was *all the faster* the car could travel.
Right: The car could not travel *faster than* forty miles an hour.

14

Errors in Punctuation

This section treats the basic errors made in punctuation. To appreciate the importance of punctuation, one need only realize that punctuation serves as a guide and as a determinant of meaning. For example, the presence of an additional comma in the second of the following sentences gives a sharply different meaning:

John, the milkman is at the door. (Direct address)
John, the milkman, is at the door. (Appositive)

187. *Periods after Common Abbreviations*

There is no rule for the use of periods with abbreviations. In many common abbreviations the period is now universally or almost universally omitted. Well-known organizations, radio stations, federal agencies, and similar groups often omit the period. Therefore, one must know the punctuation the group itself uses.

Wrong: We were listening to K.D.K.A.
Right: We were listening to KDKA.
Wrong: The ruling was handed down by the F.C.C.
Right: The ruling was handed down by the FCC.
Wrong: Mrs. Janson was active in the W.C.T.U.
Right: Mrs. Janson was active in the WCTU.

188. *Question Marks*

The question mark is used as the terminal punctuation mark in an interrogative sentence.

Is this your hat?

The question mark is used to indicate doubt about a date or other fact which has not been solidly established. This question mark is always enclosed in parentheses.

Chaucer's dates are 1340-1400 (?).

The question mark is used to produce a humorous effect. This question mark is also enclosed in parentheses.

Her hat (?) attracted considerable attention.

If a question is to be rhetorical (i.e., no answer is expected), the exclamation mark may replace the question mark.

Was ever a man so tormented!

The most common errors in using the question mark are illustrated below.

Wrong: "Is this your house?" he asked?
Right: "Is this your house?" he asked.
Wrong: Was anyone ever so lucky? (Wrong if no answer is expected.)
Right: Was anyone ever so lucky!
Wrong: Do you think we have paid too much? too little? (The phrase "too little" cannot be separated in this manner without capitalizing the word "too.")
Right: Do you think we have paid too much? Too little?
Right: Do you think we have paid too much or too little?

189. *Apostrophe To Show Possession*

The following instances illustrate the principal rules for using the apostrophe to show possession.

The apostrophe and "s" are added to singular and plural nouns to show possession.

John's book. Herbert's house. Smith's garage. Men's store. Mice's haven.

If, however, two or more persons constitute one object, only the second or last noun takes an apostrophe and "s."

Baker and Smith's store. Crosse and Blackwell's preserves. Clark, Castor, and Kline's law office.

If a singular noun ends in "s," the simple insertion of an apostrophe after the "s" is acceptable; or, if one prefers, he may add an apostrophe and "s." Hence, "Charles' task" or "Charles's task." "Jones' business" or "Jones's business."

If a plural noun ends in "s," the apostrophe is placed after the "s." Hence, "students' protest," "presidents' decisions," "boys' game."

190. *Apostrophes To Be Omitted*

Because the apostrophe and "s" have become so commonly associated with some words, the apostrophe is frequently omitted when the word becomes part of a proper noun. Examples are:

State Teachers College, Teamsters Union.

Wrong: Robinson was a Wilson State Teacher's College athlete.
Right: Robinson was a Wilson State Teachers College athlete.
Wrong: The boat approached Governors' Island.
Right: The boat approached Governors Island.
Wrong: They lived in Towsend's Inlet.
Right: They lived in Towsends Inlet.

191. *Apostrophe—To Show Plurals of Letters and Numbers*

The apostrophe must be used to form the plurals of letters and numbers.

Wrong: There were three *m*s in the word.
Right: There were three *m*'s in the word.
Wrong: There were four 90s in the scores.
Right: There were four 90's in the scores.

192. *Apostrophe—To Make Irregular Plurals*

The apostrophe is used to make plurals of words which have no standard plural form.

Wrong: I grew tired of hearing his "whens" and "wheres."
Right: I grew tired of hearing his "when's" and "where's."
Wrong: The speaker's "thems" and "thats" were quite noticeable.
Right: The speaker's "them's" and "that's" were quite noticeable.

193. *Apostrophe—Faulty Use of*

The possessive pronouns ("his," "hers," "its," "ours," "yours," "theirs," and "whose") never take the apostrophe.

Wrong: This book is *their's.*
Right: This book is *theirs.*
Wrong: The car behind the house is *our's.*
Right: The car behind the house is *ours.*
Wrong: *Who's* book is this?
Right: *Whose* book is this?

194. *Compounds—Showing Possessive in*

To make a compound possessive, add the apostrophe and "s" to the last word only. For example,

brother-in-law's, commander-in-chief's, everyone else's.

Wrong: We had his *father's-in-law* car.
Right: We had his *father-in-law's* car.
Wrong: It was *someone's else* coat.
Right: It was *someone else's* coat.

Note: If the last word in the compound ends in "s," simply add an apostrophe after the "s." For example,

sergeant-at-arms' office, keeper of the records' duties

195. *Dash—Used with an Appositive*

The dash should be used to set off an appositive that has internal punctuation.

Clouded: The newly elected leaders, John, Pete, Joe, and Herb, took office on January 3.
Clear: The newly elected officers—John, Pete, Joe, and Herb—took office on January 3.

196. *Dash—Used with a Parenthetical Element*

The dash may be used for parenthetical elements which the writer wants to emphasize.

Somewhat clouded: This report, may it never, never be forgotten, is our last, our very last.

More effective: This report—may it never, never be forgotten—is our last, our very last.

The dash may be used to set off a final short appositive.

Ineffective: He received what he asked for, nothing.
More effective: He received what he asked for—nothing.

197. *Brackets—Use of*

Brackets have three principal uses in English. The first is to enclose material which an editor or writer is inserting in a quotation. For example, the brackets in the following sentence represent an interpolation by a second writer of the word "and" into the famous line by Coleridge:

"The fair breeze blew, [and] the white foam flew"

Brackets are used to insert the name of a person reputed to be the author of a given line or longer work. For example,

The Yaller Dog
[Field]

Brackets are used to enclose the word "sic," which means that a word which appears to be a misspelling, misuse, or other deviation from correct form is printed as it is in the original. The term "sic" means "thus it is."

The letter states, "I am agin [sic] every idea you have."

Brackets must not be used loosely for parentheses.

Wrong: The captain ordered, "Batten down the hatches, and keep a sharp lookout!" [He didn't know the storm was over.]
Right: The captain ordered, "Batten down the hatches, and keep a sharp lookout!" (He didn't know the storm was over.)

198. *Capitalization of Proper Nouns*

A proper noun is the name of a specific person, place or thing. For example,

John Jameson, the President of the United States, Atlantic City, the Rock of Gibraltar.

A proper noun is always capitalized, while a common noun is not.

Wrong: john jones drove his buick to chicago, illinois.

Right: John Jones drove his Buick to Chicago, Illinois.

Note: There is a growing tendency for some persons and business houses to write their names without capitalization. For example,

> e. e. cummings, kendrick's men's shop, harrison theatre

199. Capitalization of Titles

In a title, the first word and every succeeding "main" word is capitalized.

Wrong: He was reading "the mayor of casterbridge."

Right: He was reading "The Mayor of Casterbridge."

Exception: If a word not considered a "main" word has seven or more letters, it is capitalized.

Wrong: The song was entitled "Coming through the Rye."

Right: The song was entitled "Coming Through the Rye."

200. Capitalization of Fields of Study (Subjects)

The names of fields of study which are derived from proper nouns are capitalized. If only part of the name is derived from a proper noun, only that part is capitalized.

Wrong: He was studying *spanish* and *french.*

Right: He was studying *Spanish* and *French.*

Wrong: He was studying *Early European History.*

Right: He was studying *early European history.*

Wrong: He was studying *Mathematics, Botany,* and *English.*

Right: He was studying *mathematics, botany,* and *English.*

Note: (1) the names of languages are always capitalized because they are derived from proper nouns (English, Swiss, German, Italian, etc.); (2) nouns not ordinarily capitalized (i.e., nouns not derived from proper nouns) are capitalized when they become specific course titles because they are then actually proper nouns, e.g., *Algebra 1, Basic Economics, Introduction to Geology.*

Wrong: The courses are *basic physical science, plane trigonometry,* and *english composition.*

Right: The courses are *Basic Physical Science, Plane Trigonometry,* and *English Composition.* (Right because each is the actual name of a course.)

Right: They hope to take courses in *basic physical science, plane trigonometry,* and *English composition.* (Right because in this instance they are not actually course titles.)

201. *Capitalization of Nouns and Pronouns Referring to the Deity*

Nouns and pronouns referring to the Deity are always capitalized.

Wrong: God in *his* infinite wisdom will make his decision.
Right: God in *His* infinite wisdom will make His decision.
Wrong: As Jesus entered the city, *he* saw a beggar standing in the temple.
Right: As Jesus entered the city, *He* saw a beggar standing in the temple.

202. *Quotation within a Quotation*

If a quotation appears within a quotation, the second quotation should be enclosed with single quotation marks.

Wrong: Mr. Jenks said, "I honestly believe "the money changers have fled the temple" today."
Right: Mr. Jenks said, "I honestly believe 'the money changers have fled the temple' today."

203. *Quotation Marks to Set Off Titles of Literary Works, Songs, etc.*

In days gone by, all titles were set off by quotation marks. Now, however, main titles are italicized, while titles that are part of a larger work are set off by quotation marks.

Obsolescent: He was reading "Bascom Hawke" from "Of Time and the River."
Preferred: He was reading "Bascom Hawke" from *Of Time and the River.*
Obsolescent: The tenor was singing the "Toreador Song" from "Carmen."
Preferred: The tenor was singing the "Toreador Song" from *Carmen.*

204. *Quotation Marks to Set Off Unacceptable Usage*

If one invents words or uses expressions not accepted as good usage, he should set such words and expressions off in quotation marks.

Wrong: She was *teacupping* me to death.
Right: She was *"teacupping"* me to death.
Wrong: I'm *bilin'* mad about the whole deal.
Right: I'm *"bilin'* mad"* about the whole deal.

Note: The above rule does not apply to informal writing or literary works in which informal language is used extensively, e.g., Mark Twain, Ernest Hemingway, John Steinbeck.

205. *Hyphens Used with Numbers*

The hyphen is used for compound numbers from **twenty-one to** ninety-nine.

Wrong: We had fifty four boxes in. the attic.
Right: We had fifty-four boxes in the attic.

206. *Hyphens Used with Fractions*

The hyphen is used to separate the numerator from the denominator in fractions.

Wrong: We had two thirds of a cake.
Right: We had two-thirds of a cake.

207. *Hyphens Used with Compound Modifiers*

The hyphen is used when two words not normally used **as a single** modifier are brought together for that purpose.

Wrong: It was a *Smith Jones* deal from start to finish.
Right: It was a *Smith-Jones* deal from start to finish.

208. *Hyphens Used with Certain Combinations of Letters*

The hyphen is used to avoid an awkward or perplexing **combina-**tion of letters when a prefix is used.

Wrong: We plan to *reevaluate* the situation.
Right: We plan to *re-evaluate* the situation.

Wrong: In his *preelection* speech, he made a flat promise.
Right: In his *pre-election* speech, he made a flat promise.

209. *Hyphens Used with Prefixes*

The hyphen is generally used with the prefixes "self-," "post-," "all-," "ex-," "anti-."

Wrong: He conducted a searching *selfanalysis.*
Right: He conducted a searching *self-analysis.*

210. *Hyphenated Words*

There can be no "rules" for hyphenating words because of the inconsistencies which have resulted from constantly shifting practices.

Many words which were once hyphenated no longer require the hyphen. Among the most common are

> attorney general, today, tonight, tomorrow, well travelled, nonetheless, northeaster, week end, lieutenant colonel, ill temper.

Some hyphenated words drop the hyphen when they become predicate modifiers. Among the most common of such modifiers are

> well-known, ill-bred, sub-rosa, tongue-in-cheek, fair-minded, good-natured.

Wrong: The leader was not always *well-known.*
Right: The leader was not always *well known.*
Wrong: The child was unmistakably *ill-bred.*
Right: The child was unmistakably *ill bred.*

Note: Because of constantly shifting standards, one must develop the habit of checking hyphenation in two or more dictionaries. Currently, for example, one can find two or more forms accepted by leading dictionaries for many words. Common examples are:

> *drug store* or *drugstore*   *law abiding* or *law-abiding*
> *post office* or *postoffice*   *moth eaten* or *moth-eaten*
> *safe deposit* or *safe-deposit*

211. *Commas—Errors in Use of as a Parenthetical Element*

A parenthetical element is a word or group of words that can be enclosed in parentheses because it has no grammatical bearing on the rest of the sentence. It is, in effect, an afterthought. The parenthetical element is always set off by commas and the sentence must read smoothly with the parenthetical element included or omitted. Below are examples of parenthetical elements:

> Joe, *Heaven knows how,* passed his physical education course.
>
> Our dog, *blast him,* chewed up the newspaper.

Below are examples of common errors in the use of the parenthetical element:

Wrong: He is as tall as, *if not taller,* than the teacher. (Wrong because the sentence will not read smoothly with the parenthetical element omitted.)

Right: He is as tall as, *if not taller than,* the teacher. (Right because the sentence will read smoothly with the parenthetical element omitted.)

Wrong: Chicago is as clean, *perhaps cleaner,* than Dubuque.

Right: Chicago is as clean as, *perhaps cleaner than,* Dubuque.

212. *Errors in Punctuating the Dependent Clause*

In a complex sentence that begins with the dependent clause, a comma is used to separate the dependent from the independent clause. For example,

> If he were the captain, he would be more severe.

However, if the *independent* clause opens the sentence, no comma is used.

> He would be more severe if he were the captain.

Exception: If the writer wants to emphasize the idea conveyed in the dependent clause, he may use a comma.

> He would be more severe, if he were the captain.

Wrong: The water will reflect your face, if the sun is shining brightly. (Wrong unless the writer wants to emphasize the second idea.)

Right: The water will reflect your face if the sun is shining brightly.

Wrong: Our cat will eat bread, if he is hungry. (Wrong unless emphasis is involved.)

Right: Our cat will eat bread if he is hungry.

213. *Comma—Errors in Punctuating the Appositive*

An appositive is a word or group of words having the function of identifying or pointing out. For example, in the sentence,

Washington, *capital of the United States,* is on the Potomac.

the appositive identifies the noun "Washington."

An appositive is set off by commas.

After punctuating the appositive, the writer should make certain that the sentence reads smoothly with the appositive included or removed from the sentence—just as it does in the above sentence. Otherwise, an awkward sentence structure results, as is the case with the sentence below if the appositive is removed.

Last month we saw Mr. Dreyful, *a man who has risen from the ranks,* and who is to become the president of First National.

Awkward: Finally we saw the Liberty Bell, which is Philadelphia's most prized possession, *and which* stands in the center section of Independence Hall.

Better: Finally we saw the Liberty Bell, which is Philadelphia's most prized possession, *which* stands in the center section of Independence Hall.

Awkward: This is Mr. James, who serves as my assistant, *and who* handles all matters of publicity.

Better: This is Mr. James, my assistant, *who* handles all matters of publicity.

Note: One may say: "This is Mr. James, who serves as my assistant, who handles all matters of publicity." The only objection is the repetition of the pronoun "who." This repetition is not technically incorrect; it detracts from the euphony of the sentence.

214. *Comma—Errors in Punctuating Absolute Elements*

An absolute element is a word or a group of words which has no grammatical bearing on the rest of the sentence. It must be set off by a comma.

Wrong: Our day's work done we settled down for a rest.
Right: Our day's work done, we settled down for a rest.

Wrong: The sun shining brightly it was a perfect day for sailing.
Right: The sun shining brightly, it was a perfect day for sailing.

215. *Comma—Error in Punctuating Dates and Places*

When there is more than one element in the recording of a date or a place, the elements are separated from each other by commas. For example,

> Mr. Smythe was born in *Bunting, Bardin County, Kentucky,* on *Thursday, April 12, 1922,* at a time when economic conditions were unsettled.

A common error is to omit the last comma.

Wrong: He chose *Boston, Massachusetts* for his opening address on
    Wednesday, March 8, 1961 in order to reach a wide audience.
Right: He chose *Boston, Massachusetts,* for his opening address on
    Wednesday, March 8, 1961, in order to reach a wide audience.

216. *Comma—Errors in Punctuating for Clarity*

In some situations where a comma is not normally needed, one must be used because the meaning is otherwise clouded.

Clouded: To John Parkinson's law was simply non-existent.
Better: To John, Parkinson's law was simply non-existent.
Clouded: Outside the rain was falling in torrents.
Better: Outside, the rain was falling in torrents.

217. *Comma Splice*

The so-called "comma splice" describes a common error in current writing. The term refers to the practice of separating two sentences from each other by a comma rather than by a period or semicolon. For example, the two sentences below must be treated as separate sentences; they may not be separated simply by a comma.

> The sun was shining brightly. Crowds were gathering on the beach.

The comma splice can be avoided in the manners shown below.

Wrong: The highway was very slippery, ice was to be seen everywhere.
Right: The highway was very slippery; ice was to be seen everywhere.
Right: The highway was very slippery, and ice was to be seen everywhere.
Right: The highway was very slippery. Ice was to be seen everywhere.

Note: Sometimes a parenthetical element (see page 105) appears to be a comma splice. The following are common parenthetical elements which are not comma splices.

Right: He was a genuinely good shortstop, *I believe.*
Right: He was, *I am certain,* a reliable worker.
Right: He was, *we all knew,* sincere in his efforts.

ADDENDUM

Guidelines for the use of punctuation marks are changing constantly. Therefore, the rules discussed in this section should be viewed as standards from which deviations are sometimes made.

Listed below are three departures from established rules clearly observable in the 1980s.

Many careful users of English are now leaning toward "open" punctuation.

Open punctuation is the tendency to de-emphasize the use of commas and other punctuation. Closed punctuation is the practice of adhering strictly to formal rules. In each pair of sentences below, the first sentence employs open punctuation; the second sentence employs closed punctuation.

Throughout the meeting Mary controlled her temper.
Throughout the meeting, Mary controlled her temper.

Reilly was ill, and naturally his work suffered.
Reilly was ill, and, naturally, his work suffered.

Most mass-produced labels omit all punctuation marks except capital letters.

Mr John J Sharpless	Prof Chas K Pallas
821 Long La	State Bldg
Burbank CA 91507	Brockport NY 14420

Most newspapers use individual punctuation marks—stars, asterisks, heavy type—as replacements for standard marks to gain special effects.

15

Redundancies

A redundancy is a word or expression that is so obviously in excess that it renders a sentence weak or even absurd. For example, in the following sentence,

The *wet* rain soaked us *to the skin.*

the italicized words are obviously superfluous. In fact, their presence makes the sentence ridiculous.

Difficulty in recognizing and avoiding redundancies is encountered for two reasons: (1) they are in common use in both spoken and written English and (2) some of them have become acceptable as idioms. The following sentences contain typical redundancies in everyday use:

Each person took care of his own *individual* job.

Each and *every* person is responsible for his duties.

Some redundancies acceptable as idioms are:

I am going to paint my *own* house this summer.

He *himself* will be on hand.

Both John and Mary are leaving.

This section discusses commonly found redundancies. The list, of necessity, must be partial. The reader, therefore, should begin an intensive and endless analysis of his daily use of language to eliminate redundancies, for only by such a process can he hope to free himself of one of the most common sources of errors.

218. *Any and all*

The term "any and all" is redundant because either of these words conveys the meaning by itself.

Wrong: The state will pay a bounty of $3 for *any and all* coyotes.
Right: The state will pay a bounty of $3 for coyotes (or for *any* coyote.)
Wrong: Any and *all* of the logs can be used as firewood.
Right: All the logs can be used as firewood.

219. *Combine into one*

The term "combine" means to "make one of two or more objects," "to unite," "to join." Hence the words "into one" make the phrase redundant.

Wrong: We shall *combine* the three departments *into one.*
Right: We shall *combine* the three departments.

220. *Consensus of Opinion*

Although the expression "consensus of opinion" is widely used, it is redundant because the word "consensus" means "a collective opinion."

Wrong: The president's explanation represented a *consensus of opinion.*
Right: The president's explanation represented a *consensus.*
Wrong: The *consensus of opinion* is that the defendant is guilty.
Right: The *consensus* is that the defendant is guilty.

221. *Different kinds*

Although the expression "different kinds" is used widely, there is a strong charge of redundancy against it because the word "kind" implies the word "different."

Questionable: We had four *different kinds* of soup on the menu.
Better: We had four *kinds* of soup on the menu.

Note: There can be no question of correctness of usage if the adjective "different" is modified.

The first examination was *sharply different* from the second.

222. *End result*

The use of the expression "end result" is questionable because the word "result" conveys the thought of the "end." In other words, a "result" is an "end." Therefore, speakers and writers should use a more precise term.

Poor: The *end result* was that we had no room.
Better: The *result* was that we had no room.
Poor: The *end result* of the experiment proved that we had failed.
Better: The *conclusion* of the experiment proved that we had failed.

223. *Equally as*

The word "as" used with the word "equally" creates a redundancy, and, therefore, an error.

Wrong: He is *equally as* good.
Right: He is *equally* good.
Wrong: Taylor is *equally as* strong as Peterson.
Right: Taylor and Peterson are *equally* strong.

224. *Individual person*

The word "individual" gives rise to many redundancies. The following are common examples.

Wrong: Each *individual person* must handle the question.
Right: Each *person* (or individual) must handle the problem.
Wrong: Each student must take care of his *individual self.*
Right: Each student must take care of *himself.*

225. *Needless to say*

The expression "needless to say" has come under attack by strict adherents to formal language on the grounds of redundancy because the speaker or writer who uses this phrase usually proceeds to state that which is "needless to say."

If, therefore, one wants his language to be beyond challenge, he must avoid this expression.

Questionable: Needless to say, Mother was not pleased.
Better: Naturally, Mother was not pleased.
Questionable: The outcome, *needless to say,* disturbed the president.
Better: The outcome, *as was expected,* disturbed the president.

226. *People, person*

Because many statements made in the course of a normal day pertain to people in general, the use of the words "people" and "person" frequently creates a redundancy.

Wrong: It is always enjoyable for *a person* to relax on a warm day.
Right: It is always enjoyable to relax on a warm day.
Wrong: The ocean is too cold for *people* to go swimming.
Right: The ocean is too cold for swimming.
Wrong: The *person* who is the driver must keep his eyes on the road.
Right: The driver must keep his eyes on the road.

227. *Period of time, lapse of time*

Because the words "period" and "lapse" convey the idea of time, the addition of the phrase "of time" creates a redundancy.

Wrong: We decided to stay for a short *period of time* in the little town.
Right: We decided to stay for a *short time* in the little town.
Wrong: A *lapse of time* occurred before we reached the scene.
Right: A *lapse* occurred before we reached the scene.

Note: If the amount of time involved is definitely stated, no redundancy occurs.

Right: We stayed for a period of two weeks.
Right: A lapse of ten seconds occurred.

228. *Refer back to*

The word "refer" conveys within its basic meaning the idea of "back." Therefore, the use of the word "back" with "refer" becomes redundant.

Wrong: May I refer *back to* the lines on page 10?
Right: May I refer *to* the lines on page 10?
Wrong: He referred *back to* the matter of yesterday.
Right: He referred *to* the matter of yesterday.

229. *Repeat again*

The word "repeat" means to "perform an action again." Hence, the use of "again" creates a redundancy.

Wrong: The players are going to *repeat* the performance again.
Right: The players are going to *repeat* the performance.
Wrong: He is going to *repeat* the lecture for a *second time.*
Right: He is going to *repeat* the lecture.

230. *Way, Shape, Form*

The commonly used expression, "in any way, shape, or form," is basically redundant because these terms, in most situations, are synonymous.

Wrong: He would not help us in any *way, shape* or *form.*
Right: He would not help us in any *way.*
Wrong: John does not like the idea in any *way, shape,* or *form.*
Right: John does not like the idea in any *way.*

231. *Widow woman, widower*

Because the noun "widow" can refer only to a woman, the use of the word "woman" with "widow" creates a redundancy.

Wrong: The *widow woman* entered the courtroom slowly.
Right: The *widow* entered the courtroom slowly.
Note: The adjectival form of the noun "widow" is "widowed."

Right: The recently *widowed* woman was seeking employment.
Right: The *widowed* woman was seeking employment.
Right: The woman was recently *widowed.*

From the above discussion, an important point emerges: a man whose wife has died is a "widower." However, there is no adjectival form in standard usage to correspond to this noun; that is, there is no such term as "widowered," even though the need for a term exists. ("Widowered" was once in the English language, but it faded from use.)

To meet this need, careless writers often employ this illogical and unacceptable usage:

Mr. Lowe was *widowed* in 1975 when his wife died suddenly.

To avoid the above error, the writer must resort to such a construction as:

Mr. Lowe *became a widower* in 1975 when his wife died suddenly.

16

Style

As one writes or speaks over a prolonged period, he develops certain phrases, choices of words, and rhetorical devices which are classified in writing as his "style." Consequently, for better or for worse, everyone eventually develops a style.

If one is to have an effective style, he must constantly check his writing and his speaking. He must learn to detect those shortcomings which detract from an effective style, and he must learn to capitalize upon those elements which contribute to an effective style. Thus he must constantly engage in a process of self-evaluation in order to improve his writing and his speaking.

The material in this section attempts to focus attention on improvement of style by dealing with common shortcomings.

232. *Parallelism*

Similar ideas or elements in a sentence should be phrased in a similar structural or grammatical form. If, for example, the first element is a predicate adjective, the succeeding elements also must be predicate adjectives.

Wrong: The baby was *tired, irritable,* and *needed sleep.* (Wrong because the elements are not parallel.)
Right: The baby was *tired, irritable,* and *sleepy.*
Wrong: Mr. Smithers planned on *hunting, fishing,* and *sleep.*
Right: Mr. Smithers planned on *hunting, fishing,* and *sleeping.*
Wrong: On her desk were *her books, papers,* and *the old math book.*
Right: On her desk were *her books, papers,* and *old math book.*
Wrong: I like *to swim, playing tennis,* and *riding.*
Right: I like *to swim, play tennis,* and *ride.*

Wrong: The plane *rose, leveled off,* and it *was on its way.*
Right: The plane *rose, leveled off,* and *sped on its way.*

233. *Logical Order*

The thoughts within a sentence should be arranged in logical order.

Illogical: The walls were *uneven,* the foundation was *weak,* and the whole house *showed signs of poor workmanship.*

Logical: The foundation was *weak,* the walls were *uneven,* and the whole house *showed signs of poor workmanship.* (Notice how the order proceeds from foundation to walls, to total appearance.)

Illogical: The *second man singled* after the *lead-off man doubled,* and the *third man walked.*

Logical: The *lead-off man doubled;* the *second man singled;* and the *third man walked.*

Illogical: The child *talked, stood,* and *recognized* the *neighbors* before he was nine months old.

Logical: The child *stood, talked,* and *recognized* the *neighbors* before he was nine months old.

Illogical: The contractors *applied* the *final coat* of cement and *laid* the concrete *base* on rainy days.

Logical: The contractor *laid* the concrete *base* and *applied* the *final coat* of cement on rainy days.

234. *Upside-down Subordination*

An "upside-down subordination" places the main thought in the weaker position and the secondary thought in the stronger position in a sentence.

Wrong: The boat slipped out of the harbor, when suddenly I realized I was on my way to Europe.

Right: As the boat slipped out of the harbor, I suddenly realized I was on my way to Europe.

Wrong: The plane began to lose altitude when the motor began to miss and sputter.

Right: As the motor began to miss and sputter, the plane began to lose altitude.

235. *Unrelated Thoughts*

If two or more thoughts are to be joined by coordinate conjunctions, they should be related. For example, the thoughts in the following sentence are related:

Timmy is very tired, and he really should go to bed.

If the thoughts joined by a coordinate conjunction are not related, the sentence should be recast.

Wrong: Mr. Thompson is my friend, and he is six feet tall.
Right: Mr. Thompson, my friend, is six feet tall.
Wrong: The snow was very heavy, and I am sure I don't like rain.
Right: The snow was very heavy. I should also add that I don't like rain.

236. *Loose Construction*

One must not loosely string together several ideas. Rather, he must subordinate the least important ones.

Wrong: The clock was striking seven, and the sun was shining brightly, and so I decided to arise, but I was not certain that I could do so without disturbing the family, and so I lay quietly in bed for another hour.
Right: Because the clock was striking seven and the sun was shining brightly, I decided to arise. However, not being certain that I could do so without disturbing the family, I lay quietly in bed for another hour.

237. *Sentence Fragments*

A sentence fragment is a group of words which is mistakenly punctuated as a sentence. Although established writers sometimes write sentence fragments for effect, the practice must be handled carefully in any situation and avoided in most.

Wrong: The rats along the wharf were really large. Large enough to tackle a full grown cat.
Right: The rats along the wharf were really large. They were large enough to tackle a full grown cat.
Wrong: He was late for work every morning. At least, every morning that I rode in the bus with him.

Right: He was late for work every morning. At least, he was late every morning that I rode in the bus with him.

238. *Incomplete Constructions*

In many instances in English, one may omit words because they are so clearly implied that stating them makes a sentence unnecessarily "word heavy." For example, in the following sentence the word "had" is understood:

The team had practiced and gone home.

In this instance, the auxiliary "had," which is needed for the verb phrase, "had gone," is understood because it appears in the preceding verb phrase, "had practiced." However, the practice of omitting words because they are understood, must be handled carefully. Otherwise, an error may result, as is the case in the following sentence:

The walls have been painted and the door sanded.

This sentence contains an error because the auxiliaries of the verb phrase, "have been painted," cannot be used with "sanded." The complete sentence would read

The walls have been painted and the door have been sanded.

Wrong: The old president has been defeated, and new officers elected.
Right: The old president has been defeated, and new officers have been elected.
Wrong: Patterson is to be the first choice, and Donahue and Riley the second and third.
Right: Patterson is to be the first choice, and Donahue and Riley are to be the second and the third.
Wrong: Our captain was first in the seedings, and our other two players seventh and ninth.
Right: Our captain was first in the seedings, and our other two players were seventh and ninth.

239. *Mixed Constructions*

The term "mixed construction" is self-explanatory. Note the following examples.

Mixed construction: Consider how for a moment in the problem at hand the contributing forces are involved.

Improved: Consider for a moment how the contributing forces are involved in the problem at hand.

Mixed construction: With the noise of the party still ringing in my ear, the next three traffic lights were green I noticed.

Improved: I noticed, as the noise of the party still rang in my ear, that the next three traffic lights were green.

Mixed construction: Next to the gasoline station over the hills three doors below the drug store with his three sons Mr. Hill lives in a white house.

Improved: Mr. Hill, with his three sons, lives over the hill in a white house that is located next to the gasoline station. It is three doors below the drug store.

240. *Failure to Subordinate*

If a compound sentence is used to express two ideas, the ideas are said to be "coordinated" or made equally important. For example, in the sentence,

He is tired, but he is going to New York.

the two ideas are coordinated or given equal emphasis. However, in the sentence,

Although he is tired, he is going to New York.

the first idea has been subordinated to the second.

The principle of subordination must be remembered in order to avoid excessive or illogical coordination.

Wrong: The sun was shining, and rain was falling.
Right: Although the sun was shining, rain was falling.
Wrong: He is a good worker, and I don't like him.
Right: Although he is a good worker, I don't like him.
Wrong: He is here now, and I will not speak to him.
Right: Even though he is here now, I will not speak to him.

241. *Faulty Subordination*

When an idea is to be subordinated, it must be so placed that it modifies the main thought.

Wrong: I threw the line over the side of the boat, when suddenly I remembered that the rope was fouled. (Wrong because the main thought is not modified properly.)

Right: As I threw the line over the side of the boat, I suddenly remembered that the rope was fouled.

Wrong: The plane was cruising at 5,000 feet, but the ground was clearly visible. (This sentence is grammatically correct, but neither idea is subordinated. Therefore, if subordination is desired, the sentence is wrong.)

Right: Although the plane was cruising at 5,000 feet, the ground was clearly visible.

Right: Although the ground was clearly visible, the plane was cruising at 5,000 feet.

242. *Overlapping Subordination*

If two or more ideas are to be subordinated, be careful not to let the subordination overlap.

Wrong: The captain mounted the bridge as the gale gathered force when the sailors were checking the lifeboats.

Right: As the gale gathered force and the sailors checked the lifeboats, the captain mounted the bridge.

Wrong: Mother was doing her Christmas shopping when she suddenly remembered that she needed a new broom as she entered the housewares department.

Right: When Mother was doing her Christmas shopping, she suddenly remembered as she entered the housewares department that she needed a new broom.

243. *Remote Antecedents*

The error of the "remote antecedent" results from placing so many words between a noun or a pronoun and its antecedent that the reader either has to strain to find the antecedent or the whole idea becomes vague.

Vague: The men worked their way slowly past the gaping bystanders as the first shadows of evening began to fall. They never paused, however, to check the time. (Vague because the reader has to strain to realize that the antecedent of "they" is men. The many words between the pronoun "they" and its antecedent, in addition to the presence of the word "bystanders," makes the reader strain for the meaning ot fhe sentences.)

Better: As the first shadows of evening began to fall, the men worked their way slowly past the gaping bystanders, never pausing to check the time.

Vague: The horses galloped after the baying hounds, up hill and down dale, in pursuit of the fox. Never did they seem to tire.

Better: The horses galloped after the baying hounds, up hill and down dale, in pursuit of the fox. Never did the horses seem to tire.

244. *Weak Reference*

The term "weak reference" describes a sentence in which the reader must supply the antecedent because it is not stated in the sentence.

Weak: Because we write the pupil's name on his report card, they cannot lose their reports.

Better: Because we write the pupil's name on his report card, the pupils cannot lose their reports.

Weak: In London, they drive on the left side of the road.

Better: The people in London drive on the left side of the road.

245. *Shift in Point of View*

If one uses a pronoun which has no clear antecedent, he is likely to change the point of view intended in the sentence.

Wrong: I always carry a briefcase because *they* protect my books.

Right: I always carry a briefcase because *it* protects my books.

Wrong: Let's consider the situation where *you* have to pay more taxes.

Right: Let's consider the situation where *one* has to pay more taxes.

Wrong: I don't like to hear a fire whistle blow because *they* really upset me.

Right: I don't like to hear a fire whistle blow because the *sound* really upsets me.

246. *Repetition of Words*

Unnecessary repetition should be avoided.

Poor: It was a blow *to* the Wilson School *to* lose *to* the Farson School.

Better: Losing to the Farson School was a blow to the Wilson School.

Poor: The *blowers blew blue* steam from the vents.

Better: The blowers sent blue steam from the vents.

Poor: Jimmy went *to* the baker's, *to* the shoemaker's, *to* the drug store, and *to* the grocer's.

Better: Jimmy went to the baker's, the shoemaker's, the drug store, and the grocer's.

Poor: Cantor was brash, *was* irritable, and *was* rude.

Better: Cantor was brash, irritable, and rude.

Note: Repetition, when properly used, can be effective in gaining emphasis. For example,

The car *clattered* and *clattered* down the street.

In work and *in* play, Kingston was a huge bundle of energy.

247. Superfluity

A superfluity is a word or expression which can be omitted without any loss in meaning. Although the superfluity, unlike the redundancy, is not a serious error, it should be avoided in the interest of conciseness.

Superfluous expression: When Pete and the guard were finally alone, they spoke *to each other* in a relaxed manner.

Better: When Pete and the guard were finally alone, they spoke in a relaxed manner.

Superfluous expression: The smoke from the camp fire rose softly *through the air.*

Better: The smoke from the camp fire rose softly.

Superfluous expression: He leafed through *the pages of* the book.

Better: He leafed through the book.

248. Ambiguity

An ambiguous sentence is one which logically can have two meanings.

The problem with the ambiguity is to try to determine the meaning intended by the user. For example,

Mr. Flack told his brother that he must pay the bill.

This sentence is ambiguous because it does not make clear who must pay the bill. The ambiguity arises with the use of the second "he."

Below are illustrated the principal ways to avoid ambiguity.

Ambiguous: Mother told Mary that she believes she should reduce. (Who should reduce?)

Clear: Mother told Mary, "I believe I should reduce."

Clear: Mother told Mary that she believes she (Mary) should reduce.

Ambiguous: The professor told his colleague that he must consider giving a new course.

Clear: The professor told his colleague that the colleague must consider giving a new course. (Note: some grammarians condemn this structure on the basis of the repetition of the word "colleague.")

Clear: The professor told his colleague, "I must consider giving a new course."

Clear: The professor told his colleague that he (the professor) must consider giving a new course.

249. *Shorter Expressions*

In the interest of conciseness, speakers and writers should frequently use the shorter of two or more acceptable expressions. The following pairs of sentences represent expressions that may be used interchangeably, but the shorter one is preferred if conciseness is to be gained.

Acceptable: He spoke for a *half of an hour.*

More concise: He spoke for a *half hour.*

Acceptable: Mr. Tasker gave only *part of an answer* to the question.

More concise: Mr. Tasker gave only a *partial answer* to the question.

Acceptable: Jim Kenton, *who is a neighbor of mine,* is coming with me.

More concise: Jim Kenton, *my neighbor,* is coming with me.

Acceptable: We walked over a lawn *that was covered with debris.*

More concise: We walked over a *debris-covered* lawn.

Acceptable: He spoke *in an appropriate manner* of the event.

More precise: He spoke *appropriately* of the event.

250. *Contractions in Formal Writing*

Authorities are in almost complete agreement that contractions should not be used in formal writing. They permit the use of contractions in spoken language and in personal and other kinds of informal writing. The following instances are representative of errors in formal writing.

Wrong: I *won't* be able to attend the convention next week. (Note that in this sentence the contracion "won't" is also wrong on the count that it is a contraction for "will not." If a contraction were correct, the word "shan't" would be necessary.)

Right: I *shall not* be able to attend the convention next week.
Wrong: We *don't* see the answer in sight.
Right: We *do not* see the answer in sight.
Wrong: The shipping department *won't* comply with my request.
Right: The shipping department *will not* comply with my request.

251. *Overstatement*

If one is to be precise, he must be careful of overstatement, or exaggeration. The term is self-explanatory. Essentially it reveals carelessness in the choice of words.

Wrong: *Every fan* in the ball park was thrilled with the outcome of
    the game.
Right: *Almost every fan* in the ball park appeared to be thrilled with
    the outcome of the game.
Wrong: Wagner is *everybody's choice* as the world's greatest composer.
Right: Wagner is *many persons' choice* as the world's greatest composer.
Wrong: Like *all* Welshmen, he thrills to music.
Right: Like *most* Welshmen, he thrills to music.

Note: Overstatement is permitted for light or humorous effect, as shown below:

His eyes were as powerful as an X-ray.

Our cat can eat as much as a hungry lion.

This briefcase must weigh a ton.

17

Broad and Vague Words

Careful speakers and writers do not use words which their readers or listeners may misinterpret. For example, a "good" man may be one who is moral, sound, reliable, proficient, industrious, helpful, altruistic, or pleasant. On the other hand, a "bad" man may be one who is evil, dishonest, immoral, erratic, or inefficient.

The following list of broad and vague words is very brief. It is designed merely as a basis for stimulating the reader into developing a more careful choice of words. Taking this list as a beginning, the student should proceed to evaluate the words in his vocabulary for preciseness. When he finds that he must use a broad or vague word, he should be certain to make his meaning clear.

252. *Claim*

The verb "claim" means "to demand that which has been stipulated or that which is one's right." The term should not be used as a synonym for "state," "maintain," "allege," or some similar word.

Broad: The teacher *claims* that the child was insolent.
Precise: The teacher *maintains* that the child was insolent.
Broad: He *claimed* again that he was there.
Precise: He *declared* again that he was there.

253. *Engineer*

The term "engineer" may mean one of so many occupations that speakers and writers must always clarify its meaning. An engineer, for instance, may be a driver of a fire engine, the operator of the equipment that draws a train, the man who supervises the heating and plumbing equipment for a building, a college trained specialist **who** constructs multi-million dollars dams, or one of several other **callings.**

Vague: The man who lives next door is an *engineer.*
Clear: The man who lives next door is a civil *engineer.*
Clear: The man who lives next door is the *engineer* in charge of maintenance at the court house.

254. *Get*

"Get" is extensively used as a synonym for many other words. Although it is colloquially acceptable in many instances, it should be avoided in formal speech.

Informal: We hope to *get* a few more orders next week.
Formal: We hope to *receive* a few more orders next week.
Informal: Our representative will *get* in tomorrow at 12 o'clock.
Formal: Our representative will *arrive* tomorrow at 12 o'clock.
Informal: We are certain that he will *get* over his illness.
Formal: We are certain that he will *recover* from his illness.

255. *Make*

The word "make" has become so widely used as a synonym for many words that it almost defies definition. The following instances represent excessively broad usage:

Questionable: I won't be able to *make* that conference in March.
Better: I won't be able to *attend* that conference in March.
Questionable: We are not able to *make up* our minds immediately.
Better: We are not able to *decide* immediately.

Note: The word "make" has become idiomatic in many instances. Consequently, one frequently finds that he must use this word idiomatically.

Right: The students were given a *make-up* examination.
Right: The *make-up* man was already applying the cosmetics.
Right: The disputants decided to *make up* and be friends.

256. *Possible—possibly*

The words "possible" and "possibly" are often used so loosely **that** they raise a question of logic.

Wrong: Is it *possible* to eat snake meat?
Right: Is snake meat *edible?* ("Edible" means that which a human can consume without harmful effects.)
Wrong: He came as fast as he was *possibly* able.
Right: He came as fast as he *was able.*
Wrong: We can't *possibly* have rain today.
Right: Rain today is highly *improbable.*
Wrong: That child's conduct is *impossible.*
Right: That child's conduct is *deplorable.*

257. *Professional*

The word "professional" now has so many meanings that careful speakers and writers must qualify it by definition.

Basically, the word should be applied only to a person or thought that pertains to a profession. The word "profession," however, is almost as broadly used as "professional." Whereas in days gone by, the term "profession" was limited to the church, medicine, law, teaching, and the military, the term has been appropriated by almost every other group. Consequently, one hears of the "profession" of accounting, engineering, nursing, and many, many other fields.

Questionable: He is a *professional* automobile mechanic.
Formal: He earns his living as an automobile mechanic.
Questionable: Mr. Johnson is a *professional* barber.
Formal: Mr. Johnson is a barber.

258. *Professor*

The term "professor" is often used loosely in speaking or writing of a person who teaches in a college. Actually, it should be used only for one who holds professorial rank—an assistant, associate, or full professor. It does not include those below (instructor and assistant instructor) or those outside (lecturer, etc.) the professorial rank.

Wrong: When Jim finished college, he entered graduate school and became a *professor* at the same time.
Right: When Jim finished college, he entered graduate school and became an *assistant instructor* at the same time.

Note: The above usage refers principally to the United States. In many European and other countries, private teachers of musical instrument and voice are accorded the title of "professor."

259. *Thing*

The use of the word "thing" as a broad, all-purpose word is to be deplored. Presently, the word is used so loosely that the reader or listener is often required to supply a meaning for it.

Vague: The one *thing* about him that I dislike is his overconfidence.

Better: The one *characteristic* about him that I dislike is his overconfidence.

Vague: This is the *thing* that we must consider.

Better: This is the *fact* that we must consider.

18

Miscellaneous Errors in Usage

In the course of a day, one hears and sees many errors in language that are not readily classifiable. Usually, they are errors that one has heard and seen so often that he adopts them without question.

Although some usages such as those listed below are in a state of semi-acceptance as idioms, the careful speaker and writer should avoid them.

260. *A*

The adjective (or article) "a" placed before a noun conveys the idea of "one." Therefore, it should not be omitted if one is to express himself correctly.

Wrong: I have *a* hammer and saw. (As this sentence stands, "hammer and saw" are one object.)
Right: I have *a* hammer and *a* saw.
Wrong: This company needs *a* secretary and treasurer. (Wrong if the user means two officers; right if the user means one officer.)
Right: This company needs *a* secretary and *a* treasurer.
Right: The riggers were using *a* block and tackle. (Right because a block and tackle is thought of as one object.)
Right: The old fisherman was holding *a* rod and reel. (Right because a rod and reel is thought of as one object.)
Right: This is *a* wine and sauce dish. (Right because "wine and sauce" is thought of as a unit.)

261. *Also*

The word "also" should not be inserted into a sentence needlessly.

Wrong: The child ate pie, cake, and *also* ice cream.
Right: The child ate pie, cake, and ice cream.

262. *Being that—being as how*

"Being that" and "being as how" are not considered good usage because of their vague and frequently illogical nature.

Wrong: Being that I am here, I shall do the work.
Right: Because I am here, I shall do the work.
Wrong: Being as how he owned a plane, he was able to make the trip.
Right: As he owned a plane, he was able to make the trip.

263. *But what*

The expression "but what" can be accepted, at best, as colloquial usage. Therefore, careful speakers and writers should avoid it.

Colloquial: I don't know *but what* we should paint the house.
Formal: I think that *perhaps* we should paint the house.
Colloquial: He is not sure *but what* the bearing is burned out.
Formal: He is not sure *that* the bearing is not burned out.

264. *Cannot and will not*

An instance of an error that is rarely detected by careful speakers is the expression "cannot and will not." An examination of the meaning of each part of this expression, however, immediately reveals the error, for if one "cannot" perform a given act, he obviously need not state that he "will not." The expression, therefore, represents an absurdity.

Wrong: I *cannot and will not* attend Joe's party.
Right: I *cannot* attend Joe's party. Therefore, he must not expect me.
Wrong: Our country *cannot and will not* support that measure, because morally we are unable to do so.
Right: Our country *will not* support that measure because morally we are unable to do so.

265. *Can't help but*

Although the expression "can't help but" is widely used, it is not acceptable in precise usage.

Wrong: I *can't help but* think that he must be mistaken.
Right: I *can't help* thinking that he must be mistaken.

266. *Contact*

Although the word "contact" is widely used as a verb, its use in this manner is still a matter of question. True, most authorities do not condemn this use, but some do. The careful speaker and writer, therefore, should be aware of this fact.

Questionable: I shall *contact* you early next week.
Formal: I shall *communicate* (or write, visit, etc.) *with* you early next week.
Questionable: I shall *contact* you by telephone on Friday.
Formal: I shall *call* you on Friday.

267. *Convey back*

The word "convey" means to "carry" or to "transmit." Probably because of its synonymous use with the word "carry," a tendency arises to use with it the word "back," thereby creating an error.

Wrong: Please *convey* my best wishes *back* to your parents.
Right: Please *convey* my best wishes to your parents.
Wrong: If you *convey* this suggestion *back* to your committee, we shall obtain a solution to our problem.
Right: If you *convey* this suggestion to your committee, we shall obtain a solution to our problem.

268. *Double Negative*

Although a double negative is to be found frequently in Shakespeare and other older writers, it is now considered incorrect. The double negative, as the name implies, is the use of two negatives to express a single negative idea.

Wrong: I *don't never* go swimming in September.
Right: I *never* go swimming in September.
Wrong: Lou *doesn't* want *none* of that cake.
Right: Lou *doesn't* want any of that cake.
Wrong: She *never* sees *none* of her old friends any more.
Right: She *never* sees any of her old friends any more.

269. *Double Titling*

When a person is given two or more titles, one must be careful not to let one title repeat another. The following are instances of double titling.

Wrong: We spoke with *Dr.* John K. Lanson, *M.D.* (Wrong because the degree "M.D." repeats the title "Dr.")
Right: We spoke with Dr. John K. Lanson.
Right: We spoke with John K. Lanson, *M.D.*
Wrong: The leader of the movement is *Mr.* Harold L. Paine, Esq.
Right: The leader of the movement is *Mr.* Harold L. Paine.
Right: The leader of the movement is Harold L. Paine, *Esq.*

Note: The following instances are correct because the second title does not repeat the first title.

Right: We gave the letter to Thomas Finney, D.D.S., Chairman.
Right: We gave the letter to Professor Thomas Finney, D.D.S.
Right: There is President Thomas Finney, D.D.S.
Right: We spoke with the Rev. John K. Stone, S.J., Ph.D.

270. *Etc.*

The use of the abbreviation "etc." or the longer form "etcetera" still lacks acceptance in formal writing. The objection rises from the fact that it is a broad and vague term. It is based on the assumption that the reader knows exactly what the writer is thinking. This assumption is sometimes quite sound, as in: "One, two, three, four, etc." However, the term can also be vague, as in: "We had apples, oranges, pears, etc."

Vague: The track meet will include dashes, middle distance races, long distance races, *etc.*
Better: The track meet will include dashes, middle distance races, long distance races, and four field events—the high jump, the broad jump, the pole vault, and the shot put.
Vague: We need typists, stenographers, clerks, *etc.*
Better: We need typists, stenographers, clerks, and other office personnel.

271. *Finalize*

The word "finalize" is not considered acceptable usage, despite its wide currency in the business world. It is, like many other currently popular business terms, a "fad" word.

Wrong: We are planning to *finalize* the agreement tomorrow.
Right: We are planning *to make* the agreement *final* tomorrow.
Wrong: A signature is needed to *finalize* the contract.
Right: A signature is needed *to make* the contract *legal*.

272. *Firm up*

The expression "firm up," like the word "finalize," is not considered to be acceptable. The objections are the same as those cited above.

Wrong: We are now in the process of *firming up* the contract.
Right: We are now *in* the *final stages* of making a contract.
Wrong: We hope to *firm things up* by tomorrow.
Right: We hope to *arrive at a conclusion* by tomorrow.

273. *Graduated—was graduated*

Formal usage does not sanction the verb "graduate" in the active voice to mean "successfully complete a course of study leading to a diploma or a degree." The verb, therefore, in this sense must be used in the passive voice. (See page 63 for a discussion of "passive voice.")

Wrong: Painter *graduated* from college last year.
Right: Painter *was graduated* from college last year.
Wrong: He expects to *graduate* from high school next month.
Right: He expects *to be graduated from* high school next month.

274. *Heart failure*

The term "heart failure" should not be used loosely as a synonym for death resulting from coronary ailments or diseases. As editors tell their cub reporters who use this term, "everybody dies of heart failure."

Wrong: The elderly man died suddenly of *heart failure*.
Right: The elderly man died suddenly of a coronary occlusion (or whatever other coronary condition is involved).

275. *If and when*

Because the conjunction "and" gives equal status to the elements on either side of it, the expression "if and when" creates an impossible situation. For example, in the following sentence

"If and when he comes, tell him to finish the job."

an impossible situation exists because the speaker is saying

"If he comes, tell him to finish the job."

and

"When he comes, tell him to finish the job."

Obviously, the speaker must mean one or the other, rather than both.

Wrong: *If* and *when* the cabinet acts, I shall respond accordingly.
Right: If the cabinet acts, I shall respond accordingly. (This sentence implies some doubt that the cabinet will act.)
Right: When the cabinet acts, I shall respond accordingly. (This sentence is based on the assumption that the cabinet is going to act.)

276. *In regard to—in regards to*

The word "regard" should not be used carelessly in its plural form. The word means, in most instances, "a consideration for." When one realizes the meaning, he sees immediately the error treated below.

Wrong: In *regards* to your problem, I am offering a suggestion.
Right: In *regard* to your problem, I am offering a suggestion.
Wrong: I am speaking in *regards* to the matter we discussed.
Right: I am speaking in *regard* to the matter we discussed.
Right: I am speaking *regarding* the matter we discussed.

277. *-ish—As a Suffix*

In some circles, there is a practice of attaching the suffix "-ish" to many nouns. The usage is definitely questionable in formal language.

Questionable: He is a *stand offish* person.
Better: He is an *aloof* person.
Questionable: Mrs. Stoner is *fortyish*.
Better: Mrs. Stoner is *in her forties*.

Note: The suffix "-ish" is widely accepted when attached to colors—*bluish, brownish, reddish,* etc.

278. *Kind*

The word "kind" gives rise to the two basic errors explained below. The noun "kind" is singular. Therefore, if it is to be modified by an adjective, the adjective must also be singular.

Wrong: I like *these kind* of players. (The adjective "these" is plural. Therefore, it cannot be used to modify the singular noun "kind.")
Right: I like *this* kind of player. (The adjective "this" is singular. Therefore, it is correct as the modifier of the word "kind.")

The noun in the prepositional phrase following the word "kind" is always plural, even though it may be written in the singular form. For example, in the sentence,

I like this kind of apple.

The word "apple" is plural because it is actually "apples." The fact that the word may be written in the singular form, even though it is plural, gives rise to the error discussed below.

Wrong: I like this kind of *a* car. (Wrong because there is no justification for inserting "a" before the plural word "car.")
Right: I like this kind of car.
Wrong: This is the kind of *a* day that makes me lazy.
Right: This is the kind of day that makes me lazy.

279. *Ought*

The word "ought" may not be used for the auxiliary "should" except in a dialectal sense. Naturally, one may not use dialectal speech for formal speech.

Wrong: We *ought* sharpen the axe immediately.
Right: We *should* sharpen the axe immediately.
Wrong: They *ought* buy that car.
Right: They *should* buy that car.

Note: The following are examples of the word used correctly. Note the presence of the infinitive.

We *ought* to help the chairman.

John *ought* to do his homework.

Harry *ought* to learn to drive a car.

280. *Reason is because*

The word "because" is a subordinate conjunction; it is never a relative pronoun. A very common error in grammar, however, arises from the use of the word "because" for the relative pronoun "that."

Wrong: The *reason* he came *is because* he enjoys music. (Wrong because the word "because" is used here to fill the need of a relative pronoun.)

Right: The *reason* he came *is that* he enjoys music. (Right because the word "that" is a relative pronoun.)

Wrong: The *reason* I am ill *is because* I ate too much.

Right: The *reason* I am ill *is that* I ate too much.

Right: I am ill because I ate too much. ("Because" is used correctly in this instance as a conjunction.)

Right: Because the stream is swollen by heavy rains, we must not go swimming.

281. *Seldom ever*

The speaker and the writer must be careful of the needless insertion of the word "ever" with the word seldom.

Wrong: He is *seldom ever* on time for his lectures.

Right: He is *seldom* on time for his lectures.

282. *Try and*

The conjunction "and" automatically gives equal status to the elements which it connects. For example, in the sentence,

Joe danced and sang.

equal emphasis is given to both "danced" and "sang." Because the conjunction "and" makes the elements on either side equal, the following error must be avoided:

Wrong: I shall try *and* come to your party. (This sentence is wrong because it says, "I shall try and I shall come." In other words, the speaker is promising flatly to come.)

Right: I shall try *to* come to your party. (This sentence is correct because the speaker is simply promising to try. He is not promising to come.)

Wrong: I shall try *and* skate on the rough ice.

Right: I shall try *to* skate on the rough ice.

283. *Want in—want out*

The expressions "want in" and "want out" are dialectal. Therefore, they should be avoided in formal speaking and writing.

Wrong: Kendrick *wants in* our club.

Right: Kendrick *wants to be in* our club.

Wrong: He doesn't like the army; he *wants out.*

Right: He doesn't like the army; he wants *to be discharged.*

284. *Writing of Names*

The tradition is now firmly established that every person has the right to state his preference regarding the manner in which his name is to be written. If, for example, a man wants his name written "J. Chas. Kanton," that is the manner in which it is to be written. If another person desires his full name, that form becomes the correct one. In fact, some persons have adopted initials which actually do not stand for a name, as for example, former President Harry S. Truman, whose middle initial does not stand for any name.

Care must also be exercised in the writing of parts of names which are capitalized by some owners but not by others. The following are examples of names that are not uniformly capitalized.

du Marche	di Conte
von Stassen	van Hoffer
auf der Heyde	de la Platte

Index